Conquer Grammar

Table of Contents

Capitalization

Temporal Words

Sentences

Language

Introduction

This book is designed to help students have a better understanding of grammar, the fundamental organizing principle of language. The standards for most states as well as the Common Core State Standards require that students "Demonstrate command of the conventions of standard English grammar usage when writing and speaking." Students who understand how to use proper grammar are better able to say what they mean when writing and speaking.

Each of the 84 worksheets in this book reinforces a grade-appropriate grammar topic. The book is organized by parts of speech and other key topics. The goal is to equip students with an understanding of grammar so they can communicate more effectively.

How to Use This Book

Here are just a few of the many ways you can use this resource.

Grammar Mini-Lessons: The most basic way to use this book is as a source of grammar mini-lessons. Write the grammar rule on the board. You can copy this straight from the gray box found on each worksheet. Introduce the rule, explain it, and then give examples. See if students can come up with their own examples. Then have students complete the worksheet. You can ask students to complete the worksheets individually or with partners, depending on ability levels. Check for understanding.

Grammar Reinforcement: After you have taught students a particular grammar rule, you can use these pages to give students the practice they need to reinforce their knowledge of the skill.

Grammar Assessment: The worksheets can serve as a formative assessment tool to show you where students might need additional teaching. Worksheets can also serve as a final assessment to confirm that students have mastered a particular rule.

Beyond the Book

There are myriad ways in which you can extend the lessons in this book. The goal is to keep the learning fun and interactive. Here are several ideas to get you started.

- Find examples of grammar rules you are studying in books you are reading in class. Point out these examples to students. Then send students on a scavenger hunt to find examples themselves. You can expand the search area to books students read at home and in magazines, newspapers, notices around school, advertisements—anywhere there is a written word. The more places students see the rule being used, the better.

- Ask students to practice using specific grammar rules in their own writing. For example, if you are studying a particular type of punctuation, have students use that punctuation in their writing. They can even go back and revise old work using knowledge gained from new grammar rules.

- Build a grammar "Wall of Shame" where you post examples of writing—usually from advertisements—where grammar rules were ignored, often to humorous effect. Encourage students to look for examples to add to the Wall of Shame. You might want to post an example you can easily find on the Internet, "Let's eat Grandpa" versus "Let's eat, Grandpa," and point out that grammar can save lives.

- Create a short daily exercise in which students are asked to use a recently learned grammar rule to correct a sentence that is written on the board. Students love correcting others' mistakes!

- Set up grammar stations with worksheets that cover a different rule at each station. Have students work in small groups to add one or two new questions to the worksheet at each station. Make a quiz out of the student-written questions.

Key Tips for Teaching English Learners

The rules of grammar vary between different languages. This can make learning English grammar particularly difficult for English Learners. It is helpful to know where the grammar rules between languages differ so much as to cause a fair amount of confusion. Here are some of those areas.

Word Order	In languages such as Spanish, Farsi, Arabic, and Korean, word order in sentences may vary from that of English.
Verbs	In English, verbs are inflected for person and number. (*Everyone cooks food. She has a large cat.*) Verbs are not inflected for person and number in Vietnamese, Hmong, Korean, Cantonese, and Mandarin. (*Everyone cook food. She have large cat.*)
Nouns	Nouns and adjectives use different forms in English. (*They felt safe in their home. They were concerned about safety.*) In Spanish, Hmong, Cantonese, and Mandarin, speakers use the same form for nouns and adjectives. (*They felt safety in their home.*)
Possessive Nouns	In English, we add an apostrophe and *s* to most singular nouns, or an apostrophe only to proper, plural names that end in *s*, to show possession. In Spanish, Vietnamese, Hmong, and Tagalog, possession is shown using *of*. It is always *of Holly*, not *Holly's*.
Plural Nouns	Nouns become plural after a number greater than one in English. (*We go home in two weeks. They are bringing five shirts.*) In Vietnamese, Hmong, Tagalog, Korean, Cantonese, Mandarin, and Farsi, there is no change in the noun following a number. (*We go home in two week. They are bringing five shirt.*)
Adjectives	Adjectives precede the nouns they modify in English (*the blue flower*). In Spanish, Vietnamese, Hmong, Farsi, and Arabic, adjectives follow the nouns they modify (*the flower blue*).
Pronouns	In English, there is a distinction between subject and object pronouns. (*He gave it to me. We spent time with her.*) In Spanish, Vietnamese, Hmong, Cantonese, Mandarin, and Farsi, there is no distinction. (*He gave it to I. We spent time with she.*)
Prepositions	The use of prepositions in other languages differs from those used in English. (English: *The movie is on the DVD.* Spanish: *The movie is in the DVD.*)
Articles	Indefinite articles are used consistently in English. (*She is a brilliant scientist. He is an electrician.*) In Spanish, Hmong, Tagalog, Cantonese, and Mandarin, indefinite articles can be omitted. (*She is brilliant scientist. He is electrician.*)

Name _____ Date _____

Proper Nouns

A common noun names a general person, place, or thing.

Proper nouns name specific people, places, or things.

Each main word in a proper noun should begin with a capital letter.

Common Noun	Proper Noun
girl	Darla Lopez
stadium	Yankee Stadium
ocean	Arctic Ocean

Use the chart below to sort and match each common and proper noun in the box. Write each proper noun with the correct capitalization.

country	august	jackie robinson	lake tahoe
himalayas	holiday	lake	memorial day
athlete	month	australia	mountain range

Common Nouns	Proper Nouns

Conquer Grammar • Grade 5 • © Newmark Learning, LLC

Plural Nouns

A plural noun names more than one person, place, or thing. Add **s** to the end of most nouns to make them plural. Sometimes the plural has a different ending. For nouns ending in **x**, **z**, **s**, **sh**, or **ch**, add **es**. For nouns ending in a consonant and **y**, change the **y** to **i** and add **es**.

Singular Noun	Plural Noun
lesson	lessons
lunch	lunches
class	classes

Rewrite each sentence with the plural form of the noun in the parentheses ( ).

1. (Bus) bring many of us to school.

_____

2. Today, Mrs. Davis has arranged our (desk) in a big circle.

_____

3. In the middle of the circle are several (box).

_____

4. All of the (student) wonder what the special activity will be.

_____

Circle the correct plural noun or nouns to complete each sentence.

5. Our fathers use (axs, axes) to chop some wood for our campfire.

6. My friend and I are in charge of washing the (dishes, dishs) after the meal.

7. We put up our (tentes, tents) and then look for colorful (birdes, birds) in the trees.

Name _____ Date _____

Irregular Plural Nouns

The plural form of some nouns is irregular because there are no clear spelling rules to follow when forming the plural. Sometimes a noun's spelling doesn't change at all.

Singular Noun	Plural Noun
man	men
foot	feet
die	dice

Complete each sentence with the plural form of the noun in the parentheses ( ). If necessary, use a dictionary for help.

1. The dentist cleans my _____ twice each year. (tooth)

2. My neighbors are _____ in high school. (freshman)

3. The farmer saw _____ in the barn. (mouse)

4. We played a board game that used a pair of _____. (die)

5. Thirty-eight _____ are on this field trip to the aquarium. (child)

6. Maybe we will see _____ swimming in the lake. (goose)

7. Several _____ were riding bicycles in the park. (woman)

8. How many _____ can the auditorium hold? (person)

Conquer Grammar • Grade 5 • © Newmark Learning, LLC

Name _____ Date _____

Possessive Nouns

A possessive noun tells who or what owns something.
Use **'s** to show possession for one person, place, or thing
   The **dog's** toy squeaked.

If the noun is plural and ends in an **s**, add an apostrophe **'** to show possession.
   The **girls'** dog ran around happily.

For many irregular plural nouns, add an apostrophe **'** followed by **s** to
show possession.
   The **children's** grandparents went on a trip.

**Circle the possessive noun in each sentence. Then write whether it is
singular or plural on the line.**

1. My uncle's car just pulled into the driveway. _____

2. It was a big surprise to win the contest's grand prize! _____

3. All of the tourists' luggage arrived on the following flight. _____

4. Unfortunately, the teams' jerseys were the same color. _____

5. The trees' leaves had fallen all over the yard. _____

6. The lion's roar was a hard sound to miss. _____

Name _____ Date _____

Verb Tenses

Present tense verbs tell about something that is happening right now.
Past tense verbs tell about something that has already happened.
Future tense verbs tell about something that will happen at a later time.
Use the same verb tense to describe actions that happen at the same time.
   Present: As it **starts** to rain, my dog **runs** into the house.
   Past: When the rain **stopped,** she **ran** out again.
   Future: We **will go** on a picnic tomorrow.

Write the verb in the parentheses ( ) that correctly completes the sentence.

1. When I showed up late, Mr. Turner _____ why. (wondered, wonders)

2. I shared that I _____ to the dentist the day before. (had gone, go)

3. Mr. Turner _____ me what the class was doing. (told, tells)

4. I _____ the group that was working on the science project. (join, joined)

5. Joey's grandmother _____ it to him to share with his class. (gives, gave)

6. The project isn't finished yet, but it _____ tomorrow. (will be, is)

7. We are excited to see how it _____ out. (turned, turns)

8. She handed in the test yesterday and _____ very well. (did, does)

9. We _____ a question because we felt confused. (asked, asks)

10. The audience _____ after the band played the song. (clap, clapped)

Conquer Grammar • Grade 5 • © Newmark Learning, LLC

Name _____ Date _____

Verb Tenses

Present tense verbs tell about something that is happening right now.
Past tense verbs tell about something that has already happened.
Future tense verbs tell about something that will happen at a later time.
Use the same verb tense to describe actions that happen at the same time.
   Present: When the orchestra **comes** onstage, the audience **claps**.
   Past: When the orchestra **came** onstage, the audience **clapped**.
   Future: I **will attend** the concert.

Write the verb in the parentheses ( ) that correctly completes the sentence.

1. I get stage fright every time I _____ in a piano recital.

   (will perform, perform)

2. I worked really hard and _____ this piece perfectly.

   (memorize, memorized)

3. Calvin was clapping while Dad and Mia _____ "Bravo!."

   (were shouting, are shouting)

4. By the time the performance was over, I _____.

   (have relaxed, had relaxed)

5. Even after I had left the stage, the audience still _____.

   (applauded, applaude)

6. I will continue taking lessons because I _____ how much I enjoy playing the piano.

   (realize, will realize)

7. My teacher says that she _____ another recital next spring.

   (had put on, will put on)

Name _____ Date _____

Shifts in Verb Tense

Present tense verbs tell about something that is happening right now.
Past tense verbs tell about something that has already happened.
Future tense verbs tell about something that will happen at a later time.
Change tenses to describe actions that happen at different times.
    The puppies **played** all afternoon and **are** now fast asleep.

Write the tense of each underlined verb on the lines:
present, *past*, or *future*.

1. The clouds <u>parted</u> early, and now the sky <u>is</u> filled with stars. _____ _____

2. I <u>ate</u> my dinner inside, but now I <u>stand</u> under the stars. _____ _____

3. I <u>brought</u> my flashlight because I <u>am</u> a little afraid of the dark. _____ _____

4. The grass <u>is</u> dry, although it <u>was</u> raining earlier today. _____ _____

5. My mother <u>said</u> the stars are <u>twinkling</u>. _____ _____

6. I <u>love</u> being outdoors, but I <u>will go</u> in soon. _____ _____

7. I <u>am</u> fine now, but I <u>will get</u> hungry later. _____ _____

Circle the verb in the parentheses ( ) that correctly completes the sentence.

8. We played soccer in the heat, and now we (are, is) exhausted.

9. Today was very hot, but we hope tomorrow (will be, can) cooler for the big game.

10. I rode my skateboard earlier, and now I (are, am) home.

11. We finished our homework, so now we (go, will go) swimming.

12. I just started watching the movie, and I (will finish, finish) it tonight.

Conquer Grammar • Grade 5 • © Newmark Learning, LLC

Name _____ Date _____

Shifts in Verb Tense

Present tense verbs tell about something that is happening right now.
Past tense verbs tell about something that has already happened.
Future tense verbs tell about something that will happen at a later time.
Change tenses to describe actions that happen at different times.
   The people who **arrived** this morning **are** still here.
   When it **gets** dark, we **will go** home.

Underline the two verbs that shift tenses in each sentence.

1. The fire crackled loudly earlier, but now it just burns quietly.

2. We overcooked our marshmallows, but we will eat them anyway.

3. We have some pineapple juice left, although we consumed a lot of it already.

4. We will sing songs later that are camp favorites.

**Rewrite each sentence with the correct form of the verb
in the parentheses ( ).**

5. Our cabin leader will tell us a story before we (go, went) to sleep.

_____

6. We request spooky stories even though they (scared, might scare) all of us.

_____

7. I went to the deli to (buy, bought) some sandwiches.

_____

8. When I get home, I will wash the tomatoes and (made, make) a salad.

_____

9. Yesterday, I (cooked, cook) spaghetti sauce that we (will use, use) tonight.

_____

10. Rob went to the restaurant and (picks, will pick) up his take-out order.

_____

Shifts in Verb Tense

Present tense verbs tell about something that is happening right now.
Past tense verbs tell about something that has already happened.
Future tense verbs tell about something that will happen at a later time.
Change tenses to describe actions that happen at different times.
    The coaches **are** so surprised that we **lost** the game.
    Our team **will practice** more than we **did** before.

**Rewrite each sentence with the correct form of the verb
in the parentheses ( ).**

1. I will play tag with my friends until it (gets, got) dark.

_____

2. When I yell my dog's name, he (will come, came) running to me.

_____

3. It was overcast, and now it (is, was) raining.

_____

4. Because it is raining, we (go, will go) back home.

_____

5. My dog chased a squirrel, so she (is, was) worn out now.

_____

6. I ran too much, so now my shins (are hurting, were hurting).

_____

7. We are extremely happy that the home team (wins, won).

_____

Shifts in Verb Tense

Present tense verbs tell about something that is happening right now.
Past tense verbs tell about something that has already happened.
Future tense verbs tell about something that will happen at a later time.
Change tenses to describe actions that happen at different times.
   The children **planted** seeds that **will grow** into flowers this spring.

Rewrite each sentence with the future tense of the verb in the parentheses ( ).

1. He is out for a walk, but soon he (run).

_____

2. After he runs around the block ten times, he (stop).

_____

3. The exercise he gets from running (help) him concentrate.

_____

4. If I do extra chores, I (earn) more spending money.

_____

5. I (finish) washing dishes before I watch a movie.

_____

Rewrite each sentence. Use the correct tense for each verb in the parentheses ( ).

6. I (work) hard today, so I (rest) well tonight.

_____

7. Tomorrow, Andre (practice) before he (play) at the piano recital.

_____

Present Perfect Tense

The present perfect tense tells about an action that starts in the past and ends in the present. It can also tell about changes or experiences that happen over a period of time. The present perfect tense uses the helping verb **has** or **have** with the past participle of the main verb.

Sun Yen **has played** soccer for three years.

We **have played** on the same soccer team for all three years.

Rewrite each sentence with the present perfect tense of the verb in the parentheses ( ).

1. I (like) studying with Anna this semester.

_____

2. I (walk) to school with Felix every day this week.

_____

3. Our class (perform) in the talent show every year.

_____

4. Mr. Alvarez (coach) the chess club ever since I joined.

_____

5. I (love) Frank's banana bread for the last year.

_____

6. Beatrice (want) to become an author for a long time, and we (encourage) her.

_____

Present Perfect Tense

The present perfect tense tells about an action that starts in the past and ends in the present. It can also tell about changes or experiences that happen over a period of time. The present perfect tense uses the helping verb **has** or **have** with the past participle of a main verb.

Rosaria **has loved** to garden all her life.

Andy and Eddie **have played** the flute since last summer.

Rewrite each sentence with the perfect tense of the verb in the parentheses ( ).

1. I (help) my grandmother bake since I was very young.

_____

2. If your brother (finish) writing his story, may I read it?

_____

3. We (climb) to the peak of Mt. Charles twice.

_____

4. Mark and Eduardo (attend) the same summer camp for two years in a row.

_____

5. Mr. Singh (travel) to Toronto several times.

_____

6. I (decide) to host a party.

_____

7. We (work) on archiving the documents for a five months now.

_____

8. My sister (plays) softball for four years.

_____

Name _____ Date _____

Perfect Tenses

The present perfect tense tells about an action that starts in the past and has not yet ended. It can also tell about changes over time and life experiences. The present perfect tense uses the helping verb **has** or **have** with the past participle of a main verb.

Present perfect: Davin **has played** the drums and piano since October.

The past perfect tense tells about an action that starts and ends in the past. The past perfect tense uses the helping verb **had** with the past participle of a main verb.

Past perfect: Before that, he **had played** the violin and guitar.

The future perfect tense tells about an action that starts in the past and ends in the future. The future perfect tense uses the helping verbs **will have** with the past participle of a main verb.

Future perfect: By next year, he **will have played** four instruments.

Rewrite each sentence. Use the perfect tense in the parentheses ( ) for the underlined verb.

1. My mom <u>cook</u> lasagna since I was little. (present perfect)

_____

2. She <u>learn</u> to cook before I was born. (past perfect)

_____

3. Mom <u>boil</u> about 100 pots of water by the end of this year! (future perfect)

_____

4. My mom <u>dream</u> of opening a restaurant for a long time. (present perfect)

_____

5. I <u>hope</u> for a clothing store instead of a restaurant. (past perfect)

_____

6. I <u>start</u> drawing at the age of three. (past perfect)

_____

7. My parents <u>watch</u> all of my games this year. (future perfect)

_____

Subject-Verb Agreement

The subject of a sentence is a noun that tells who or what the sentence is about. The verb tells what the subject does. The subject and the verb in a sentence must agree. A singular subject takes a singular verb. A plural subject, including a compound subject, takes a plural verb.

Singular Subject: He **is** a good painter.
Plural Subject: A bird and a squirrel **live** in that big tree.

**Complete each sentence. Choose the verb in the parentheses ( )
that agrees with the subject of the sentence and write it on the line.**

1. Some of my neighbors _____ a community garden.

(have, has)

2. Ms. Consuelos _____ the work in the garden.

(organize, organizes)

3. However, many gardeners _____ in its care.

(share, shares)

4. In the spring, several folks _____ different kinds of seeds.

(buy, buys)

5. This year, they _____ to plant both vegetables and flowers.

(has voted, have voted)

6. I _____ cucumber seeds.

(am planting, are planting)

7. Robert and Mary _____ watermelons!

(is growing, are growing)

8. The garden _____ a great way to bring our community together.

(have been, has been)

Subject-Verb Agreement

The subject of a sentence is a noun that tells who or what the sentence is about. The verb tells what the subject does. The subject and the verb in a sentence must agree. A singular subject takes a singular verb. A plural subject, including a compound subject, takes a plural verb.

Singular Subject: The <u>boy</u> **swims** in the pool.
Plural Subject: <u>Toy boats</u> **float** nearby.

For each sentence, write *Yes* if the subject and verb agree.
Write *No* if the subject and verb do not agree and then rewrite the sentence correctly.

1. _____ My classmates and I does a lot of homework.

_____

2. _____ Denessa jogs two miles every Tuesday and Thursday after school.

_____

3. _____ I likes to play tennis at our town's tennis courts.

_____

4. _____ Most kids in my class has joined one of the clubs at school.

_____

5. _____ I see that many parents enjoy it, too.

_____

6. _____ My mom and my aunt practices yoga together on Saturday mornings.

_____

7. _____ Yoga make them feel calm and focused.

_____

8. _____ They also practice meditation at home.

_____

Subject-Verb Agreement

The subject of a sentence is a noun that tells who or what the sentence is about. The verb tells what the subject does. The subject and the verb in a sentence must agree. A singular subject takes a singular verb. A plural subject, including a compound subject, takes a plural verb.

Singular Subject: <u>He</u> **is** a good painter.
Plural Subject: The <u>trees</u> in the park **are** beautiful.

Rewrite each sentence with correct subject-verb agreement.

1. A lion are coming out from behind the tree.

_____

2. We needs to get out of here right now!

_____

3. That aren't a lion after all.

_____

4. That shadow look like an animal.

_____

5. We doesn't need to escape.

_____

6. We is still safe.

_____

7. We can eats our food now and enjoy it.

_____

Subject Pronouns

A pronoun is a word that takes the place of a noun. **I**, **you**, **she**, **he**, **it**, **we**, and **they** are subject pronouns. Use a subject pronoun when a pronoun is the subject of a sentence.

> **Incorrect: Him** is my teacher.
> **Correct: He** is my teacher.

> **Incorrect:** My sister and **me** go skating on weekends.
> **Correct:** My sister and **I** go skating on weekends.

Circle the correct subject pronoun in the parentheses ( ) to complete each sentence.

1. (They, Them) went to the movies and sat in the first row.

2. Chris and (I, me) will go to the game with you next week.

3. (Him, He) and (me, I) made it to the dance finals.

4. (Her, She) and Justine are sailing in the bay.

Underline each incorrect pronoun. Then rewrite the sentence with the correct subject pronoun.

5. Us and our cousins go fishing at the lake.

_____

6. Gino and me both sing in a choir.

_____

7. Sara and him made a pizza.

_____

8. My friend and me tutor younger students.

_____

Conquer Grammar • Grade 5 • © Newmark Learning, LLC

Object Pronouns

A pronoun is a word that takes the place of a noun. **Me, you, him, her, it, us,** and **them** are object pronouns. Use an object pronoun when a pronoun is the object of a verb or a preposition.

Incorrect: The music teacher gave an award to Laila and **I**.
Correct: The music teacher gave an award to Laila and **me**.

Incorrect: This is a key competition for us and **they**.
Correct: This is a key competition for us and **them**.

Circle the correct object pronoun in the parentheses ( ) to complete each sentence.

1. James rides the roller coaster with my sister and (I, me).

2. The rain delayed the game between (we, us) and (them, they).

3. Ariel made cookies for you and (we, us).

4. Postcards arrived for both (he, him) and his brother.

Underline each incorrect pronoun. Then rewrite the sentence with the correct object pronoun.

5. Melanie went to the concert with Taryn and I.

_____

6. The teacher gave he and her a surprise quiz.

_____

7. Andrew brought Natalie and I some popcorn.

_____

8. Please remember to call they tomorrow.

_____

Possessive Pronouns

A possessive pronoun shows that something belongs to a person or thing. The possessive pronouns are **my**, **mine**, **your**, **yours**, **her**, **hers**, **his**, **its**, **our**, **ours**, **their**, and **theirs**. A possessive pronoun never has an apostrophe.

This is not **my** jacket. That blue one is **mine**.
This book is **hers**. I'm taking it back to **her** house.

Circle each correct possessive pronoun in the following sentences.

1. The cat chased (its, their) toy mouse.

2. I finished writing (mine, my) report. Are you done with (your, yours)?

3. We can meet at (your, yours) apartment or (our, ours).

4. That red folder is (my, mine), but the purple one is (her, hers).

5. The three classmates decided to study at the library before (their, theirs) test.

6. Jenny opened the window of (her, its) car.

7. Jason, is this backpack (yours, your) or (mine, my)?

8. If you'd like to borrow (my, mine) scooter, please return it in an hour.

Interrogative Pronouns and Relative Pronouns

Use an interrogative pronoun, such as **who**, **whom**, **what**, **which**, and **whose** to introduce a question.

Use a relative pronoun such as **who**, **whom**, **whose**, **that**, and **which** to introduce a relative clause that tells more information about a word in the sentence.

Interrogative pronouns: What are your plans tomorrow? **Which** exhibit would you like to see? **Who** else would like to come? **Whose** mom is taking us to the museum?

Relative pronouns: The 3-D movie, **which** my sister has seen, is very good. My friend **who** lives around the corner may be late. We can wear the friendship bracelets **that** you made.

Circle the correct interrogative pronoun in ( ) and the correct relative pronoun in ( ) to complete each sentence.

1. (Who, What) wants to see the play (whom, that) Alejandro recommended?

2. (Which, Who) dog is the one (which, that) buried the bone?

3. (Who, Whose) wants to surf at Mission Beach, (which, who) happens to be my favorite beach?

4. (Whose, Who) recreation center is the one (whose, that) has a swimming pool?

5. (What, Which) friend is the one (that, who) plays soccer with you?

6. (Who, What) would like the extra apple (whose, that) I brought?

Name _____ Date _____

Pronoun-Antecedent Agreement

The noun that a pronoun replaces is called an antecedent. A pronoun and its antecedent must match in number and person.

Incorrect: Before **Tim** gets lost, **they** should check a map.
Correct: Before **Tim** gets lost, **he** should check a map.

Read each sentence and circle the pronoun that is correct in number.

1. You should proofread (you, your, yours) book report before you turn it in.

2. Nina and I brought (their, she, our) sleeping bags for the slumber party.

3. The fifth grade classes had a meeting about (its, their, they) bake sale.

4. After a nap, the cat found (theirs, their, its) toy and began to play.

5. This time, the parents agreed with (his, her, their) children.

6. At (its, yours, his) last rehearsal, the school choir held auditions for the big solo.

7. Dina and Dana were late for practice because (we, she, they) forgot to set the alarm.

8. Justin read a biography about (himself, he, his) favorite musician.

Conquer Grammar • Grade 5 • © Newmark Learning, LLC

Pronoun-Antecedent Agreement

The noun that a pronoun replaces is called an antecedent. A pronoun and its antecedent must match in number and person.

	Pronoun	Antecedent	Agreement
I hung the coat in **my** closet.	my	I	singular, first person
Kendra, here is **your** notebook.	your	Kendra	singular, second person
The **citizens** wanted to help, so **they** organized a community clean-up day.	they	Citizens	plural, third person

Write the pronoun that correctly completes the sentence.

1. The newest member of team, Lucy, gave _____ best effort yet.

2. The judges could not agree on _____ choice for first place.

3. You should think about the consequences of _____ actions.

4. Alaska is the largest state by area, but _____ does not have the largest population.

5. If people work together, _____ should finish the job quickly.

6. It was raining when Mark realized that _____ had forgotten an umbrella.

Name _____ Date _____

Adjectives

Adjectives are words that describe nouns. They tell about size, color, number, and kind. Follow this order when using more than one adjective to describe a noun: number (eight, many), opinion (kind, funny, tasty), size (huge, small), looks/feels (shiny, soft), age (new, ancient), color (red, yellow), origin (American, Mexican), material (metal, cotton). Place a comma after each adjective, except a number and between the last adjective and the noun.

Incorrect: We have **two, energetic, young** puppies with **long, fuzzy,** ears.

Correct: We have **two energetic, young** puppies with **long, fuzzy** ears.

Complete each sentence. Write the adjectives in the parentheses ( ) in the correct order.

1. The _____, _____, _____ bunny wiggled its nose at me.
   (fluffy white cute)

2. Did you see the _____, _____ flowers in the garden?
   (colorful tall)

3. I ordered a _____, _____, _____ pizza.
   (big Italian tasty)

4. Tony got a _____, _____, _____ bike for his birthday.
   (red wonderful shiny)

5. A _____, _____ bird flew in front of me.
   (striped small)

6. Did anyone sit on the _____, _____, _____ sofa?
   (white fancy new)

Name _____ Date _____

Adjectives

Adjectives are words that describe nouns. They tell about size, color, number, and kind. Follow this order when using more than one adjective to describe a noun: number (four, few), opinion (beautiful, special), size (tiny, wide), looks/feels (warm, bumpy), age (new, old), shape (oblong, pointed) color (gray, blue), origin (Alaskan, Egyptian), material (paper, glass). Place a comma after each adjective, except a number and between the last adjective and the noun.

> **Incorrect:** I have **two, furry, amazing, large,** dogs.
> **Correct:** I have **two amazing, large, furry** dogs.

Circle the adjectives that are in the correct order. Rewrite the adjectives on the line with commas.

1. Mike always takes his _____ bag to the gym.
   a. practical black canvas   **b.** black practical canvas

2. I'm going to cook_____ steaks.
   a. delicious thick two   **b.** two delicious thick

3. We saw a film about _____ children who live in Chicago.
   a. five teenage smart   **b.** five smart teenage

4. We bought _____ towels for our beach vacation.
   a. three fluffy multicolored **b.** multicolored fluffy three

5. Junior took pictures of _____ whales.
   a. several enormous gray **b.** several gray enormous

6. The mural is made of _____ tiles.
   a. many smooth glass small   **b.** many small smooth glass

Adjectives

Adjectives are words that describe nouns. They tell about size, color, number, and kind. Follow this order when using more than one adjective to describe a noun: number (nine, many, several), opinion (honest, friendly), size (titanic, microscopic), looks/feels (sticky, prickly), age (recent, modern), shape (round, triangular), color (pastel, translucent), origin (Chinese, Kenyan), material (straw, wooden). Place a comma after each adjective, except a number and between the last adjective and the noun.

Incorrect: My dog Jackson wore **two, old, red, cotton,** bandannas.
Correct: My dog Jackson wore **two old, red, cotton** bandannas.

Add the given adjectives to each sentence. Write them in the correct order with commas.

1. I need to return the _____ books to the library.

thick   musty   three   old

2. Beau and Jasper are Uncle Larry's _____ hounds.

spotted   curious   two

3. I placed _____ seeds in my garden.

round   many   tiny

4. The reporter interviewed _____ residents of the neighborhood.

four   longtime   concerned

5. The sun looked like a _____ ball against the evening sky.

orange   round   sizzling

6. The _____ calves stood up in the pasture.

newborn   awkward   two

Name _____ Date _____

Adverbs

Adverbs give more information about where or when an action occurs or how it happens. An adverb can appear before or after the verb it modifies or in between different verb parts.

Where: Our neighbors came **around** for a party.
When: Soon, summer will be over.
How: The sun was still shining **brightly** in the sky.

Circle the adverb in each sentence. Then write if it shows where, when, or how the action happens.

1. The athletes ran quickly around the oval track. _____

2. We sat uncomfortably on the hard, metal bleachers. _____

3. Thanks to the wind, leaves were blowing everywhere. _____

4. The team competes at track meets weekly. _____

5. The fans cheer loudly for their favorite competitors. _____

6. Later, we will share a pizza with our friends. _____

7. Yesterday, I got a haircut. _____

8. The team met eagerly at the finish line. _____

Relative Adverbs

A relative adverb introduces a relative clause and refers to a time, a place, or a reason. The relative clause gives more information about a word or phrase in the sentence. The words **when**, **where**, and **why** may be used as relative adverbs.

Time: June is usually the month **when** the rose bushes bloom.
Place: Minnesota is **where** my cousins live.
Reason: I know the reason **why** I am so tired today.

Underline the relative clause in each sentence. Circle the relative adverb.

1. Our father explained the reason why our family was moving.

2. I went to camp, where I learned to ride a horse.

3. Last year was when my sister started kindergarten.

4. Tuesday is when I have my trumpet lesson.

5. Florida is where my grandparents live.

6. I'll always remember when I lost my first tooth.

Name _____ Date _____

# Prepositions

A preposition shows the relationship between a noun or pronoun and another word in a sentence. The relationship may show **what**, **when**, **where**, or **how**. Some common prepositions are **about**, **above**, **across**, **after**, **against**, **around**, **at**, **before**, **behind**, **below**, **beside**, **between**, **by**, **during**, **for**, **from**, **in**, **near**, **of**, **on**, **out**, **over**, **through**, **to**, **under**, **until**, **up**, **with**.

The cat napped **after** <u>his meal</u>.
The book is **on** <u>the table</u> **beside** <u>the lamp</u>.

Underline the prepositions in each sentence.

1. We went hiking with our parents.

2. James walked under the trees, which were green and leafy.

3. The pollen flew around us, and it drifted into my nose.

4. At the store, Franklin found the muffin mix above the regular flour.

5. In the next aisle, beside the apples, we found the lemons.

Complete each sentence with a preposition that matches the relationship in the parentheses ( ).

6. They'll go home on the bus _____ the movie ends. (when)

7. The dog was hiding _____ the chair. (where)

8. Our class is making bridges _____ glue and craft sticks. (how)

Name _____ Date _____

Prepositions

A preposition shows the relationship between a noun or pronoun and another word in a sentence. The relationship may show **what**, **when**, **where**, or **how**. Some common prepositions are **about**, **above**, **across**, **after**, **against**, **around**, **at**, **before**, **behind**, **below**, **beside**, **between**, **by**, **during**, **for**, **from**, **in**, **near**, **of**, **on**, **out**, **over**, **through**, **to**, **under**, **until**, **up**, **with**.

After <u>lunch</u>, I'll return **with** <u>treats</u>.

Underline the prepositions in each sentence.

1. After dinner, we took our three dogs for a walk.

2. They ran down the block and around our corner.

3. They stopped beside a bush near a fence.

4. We ran toward them, and they gazed at us hopefully.

5. We reached for some treats in our bag, and the dogs jumped with joy.

Complete each sentence with a preposition that matches the relationship in the parentheses ( ).

6. Bella carried the trunk _____ the stairs to the attic.   (where)

7. Do you want to go to the library _____ lunch or after lunch?   (when)

8. Junior drove carefully into a parking space _____ two parked cars. (where)

9. I strolled _____ the bookstore.   (where)

10. I read _____ great interest.   (how)

Name _____ Date _____

Prepositions

A preposition shows the relationship between the noun or pronoun and another word in the sentence. The relationship may show **what, when, where, how,** or **how long**. Some common prepositions are **above, about, across, after, around, at, before, between, by, down, for, in, into, on, of, to, toward, under, up, at,** and **with**.

I saw a pair **of** goats running **around** a fenced-in field.
I watched them **for** a few minutes.

Circle the preposition in each sentence and underline the noun phrase that relates to the preposition.

1. Marley took us into the living room.

2. She told us about her new puppy.

3. The kitten, named Baxter, was curled up under a desk.

4. Tail wagging, Baxter barked at us.

Complete each sentence with a preposition that matches the relationship in the parentheses ( ).

5. We will have a celebration _____ the park. (where)

6. All the classes will go to Sunset View Park _____ bus. (how)

7. We'll get there _____ 10 a.m. and 10:15 a.m. (when)

8. We'll barbecue and play games _____ a few hours. (how long)

Prepositions

A preposition shows the relationship between a noun or pronoun and another word in a sentence. The relationship may show **what**, **when**, **where**, or **how**. Some common prepositions are **about**, **above**, **across**, **after**, **against**, **around**, **at**, **before**, **behind**, **below**, **beside**, **between**, **by**, **during**, **for**, **from**, **in**, **near**, **of**, **on**, **out**, **over**, **through**, **to**, **under**, **until**, **up**, **with**.

Christina walked **through** <u>the narrow opening</u>.

Circle the preposition in each sentence and underline the noun that relates to the preposition.

1. Marco appeared in the talent show.

2. He had news about a holiday sale at the mall.

3. School buses were parked behind the cafeteria.

4. We have math class after lunch.

Write the correct preposition to complete each sentence.
Then underline the noun phrase that relates to the preposition.

5. We read a story _____ the Great Blizzard.

6. The storm began _____ March 11, 1888.

7. It snowed _____ three days.

8. The river was frozen _____ thick ice.

9. Therefore, people were able to walk _____ the river.

10. Some snowdrifts lasted _____ July 4!

Name _____ Date _____

Prepositions

A preposition shows the relationship between a noun or pronoun and another word in a sentence. The relationship may show **what**, **when**, **where**, or **how**. Some common prepositions are **about**, **above**, **across**, **after**, **against**, **around**, **at**, **before**, **behind**, **below**, **beside**, **between**, **by**, **during**, **for**, **from**, **in**, **near**, **of**, **on**, **out**, **over**, **through**, **to**, **under**, **until**, **up**, **with**.

My dog curled up **beside** me **on** the couch.

Write a preposition or prepositions to complete each sentence. Choose one of the following: *from, with, at, into, through, for*.

1. I went _____ my friend Lee to the mall.

2. We were coming _____ his house.

3. As we walked _____ the door of one store, we heard a bell ring.

4. The clerk working _____ the counter greeted us.

5. We went to the sweater section _____ the back of the store.

6. We selected what we needed _____ the racks and brought it _____ the fitting room.

7. Then, I looked _____ my backpack, searching _____ my money.

8. Oh, no! I must have left my wallet _____ Lee's house.

9. I should have remembered to bring it _____ me.

10. Lee got his wallet _____ his pocket.

Correlative Conjunctions

Correlative conjunctions always come in pairs and appear in different parts of a sentence. They work together to connect the parts of the sentence. Use the correlative conjunctions **both...and** to add one idea to another. **Either...or** gives an alternative. **Neither...nor** gives no alternative. **Not only...but also** contrasts two ideas.

> We'll go **either** to a cafeteria **or** to a restaurant.
> **Both** my cousin **and** my sister came with me to the movies.
> **Neither** my sister **nor** my cousin liked the movie.
> They said they had wasted **not** one **but** two weeks of allowance.
> They were **not only** frustrated **but also** irritated.

Underline the correlative conjunctions in each sentence.

1. You can either play volleyball or swim laps in the pool.

2. The event will be both more meaningful and more enjoyable if you join us.

3. We will go neither to the skating rink nor to the bowling alley.

4. We will go either to the zoo or to the amusement park.

5. Not only will you learn something, but also you will ace the test.

Rewrite each pair of sentences as one sentence. Use the correlative conjunctions in the parentheses ( ).

6. Tessa likes historical fiction. Tessa also likes tall tales.   (both...and)

_____

7. Gabby can bring pasta salad. Gabby can bring macaroni and cheese.   (either...or)

_____

Name _____ Date _____

Correlative Conjunctions

Correlative conjunctions always come in pairs and appear in different parts of a sentence. They work together to connect the parts of the sentence.
Use the correlative conjunctions **both...and** to add one idea to another.
Either...or gives an alternative. **Neither...nor** gives no alternative.
Not only...but also contrasts two ideas.

> **Both** Morgan **and** Lucy want a pet.
> **Either** a cat **or** a dog would make a good pet.
> **Neither** Morgan **nor** Lucy has time to walk a dog.
> They adopted a cat that's **not only** beautiful **but also** friendly.

In each sentence, determine the missing half of the correlative conjunction. Write the missing part on the line to complete the sentence.

1. We'll either all take a bus _____ we'll all bike to the park.

2. _____ Suzette and Louis are going to be there later.

3. The party invitation said not to bring gifts _____ instead to make homemade cards or treats.

4. Neither the popcorn you're bringing _____ the lemonade will spoil if left out.

5. Both the food _____ the cards are on the table.

6. We will see not only our friends_____ our family!

7. _____ Rowena nor Anthony will be able to come.

8. _____ Marianne nor Mike are driving hours to be there.

Correlative Conjunctions

Correlative conjunctions always come in pairs and appear in different parts of a sentence. They work together to connect the parts of the sentence.
Use the correlative conjunctions **both...and** to add one idea to another. **Either...or** gives an alternative. **Neither...nor** gives no alternative. **Not only...but also** contrasts two ideas.

I can wear **either** shorts **or** jeans to play many sports.
I can wear **neither** shorts **nor** jeans to my uncle's wedding.

Write two sentences to answer each question. Use the correlative conjunctions *either...or* **in the first sentence and** *neither...nor* **in the second sentence.**

1. Do you want a hamburger? Do you want a hot dog?

_____

_____

2. Should we go to the beach or to the mountains?

_____

_____

Rewrite each pair of sentences with the correlative conjunctions *either...or* **or** *neither...nor***.**

3. A prairie dog is not a dog. It is not a gopher.

_____

4. They do not bark. They do not squeak.

_____

5. Prairie dogs yip. They whistle too.

_____

6. Prairie dogs move into existing burrows. Prairie dogs dig new ones.

_____

Name _____ Date _____

Correlative Conjunctions

Correlative conjunctions always come in pairs and appear in different parts of a sentence. They work together to connect the parts of the sentence.
Use the correlative conjunctions **both...and** to add one idea to another.
Either...or gives an alternative. **Neither...nor** gives no alternative.
Not only...but also contrasts two ideas.

I like **both** jam **and** jelly.
Either butter **or** tomato sauce would taste good on the pasta.

Rewrite each pair of sentences as one sentence. Use the correlative conjunctions in the parentheses ( ).

1. At the bakery, the smell of bread was savory. The smell was strong. (both...and)

_____

2. Sherry offered us cider. Sherry offered us lemonade. (either...or)

_____

3. They would like the salad. I would like the soup. (not only...but also)

_____

4. When they left, they were not thirsty. They were not hungry. (neither...nor)

_____

5. This field trip was informative. It was fun. (not only...but also)

_____

Correlative Conjunctions

Correlative conjunctions always come in pairs and appear in different parts of a sentence. They work together to connect the parts of the sentence.
Use the correlative conjunctions **both...and** to add one idea to another.
Either...or gives an alternative. **Neither...nor** gives no alternative.
Not only...but also contrasts two ideas.

Both Rosie **and** Manny came to the movies with us.
Afterward, we had **not only** pizza **but also** dessert.

Join each pair of independent clauses with the correlative conjunctions in the parentheses ( ). Write the sentence on the line.

1. Sunday was sunny. It was breezy. (both...and)

_____

2. We could go to the beach. We could fly a kite. (either...or)

_____

3. Luca did not want to fly a kite. Max did not want to fly a kite. (neither...nor)

_____

4. At the beach, I swam. I flew the kite along the shore. (both...and)

_____

5. I had a delightful day. I got a lot of exercise. (not only...but also)

_____

6. I was exhausted. I was hungry. (not only...but also)

_____

Commas for Introductory Phrases

When a sentence begins with an introductory phrase, use a comma to set off the phrase from the rest of the sentence.

At dawn, we could hear the birds begin to sing.

Underline the introductory phrase in each sentence.

1. Before I go, I should make sure I have everything with me.

2. After school, let's eat a snack.

3. Since I am hungry now, I already have something prepared.

4. Because of the time, we should probably catch the bus soon.

5. As he was the first person in line for the movie, Clarence had his choice of seats.

6. In the center section, he'll have the best view of the screen.

Rewrite each sentence. Add a comma to set off the introductory phrase.

7. Even with Patrice's goal the team lost the playoff game.

_____

8. Next season we'll do better.

_____

Commas for Introductory Phrases

When a sentence begins with an introductory phrase, use a comma to set off the phrase from the rest of the sentence.

Most years, the cherry trees are in full bloom in April.

Rewrite each sentence. Add a comma to set off the introductory phrase.

1. In my opinion the ballet performance was lovely.

_____

2. In fact the whole audience seemed to agree.

_____

3. In the beginning I wasn't sure that the ballerinas would be good.

_____

4. However I was so wrong!

_____

5. During intermission two young ballerinas peeked out from behind the curtain.

_____

6. At the end some fans tossed single roses onto the stage.

_____

7. Honestly it was the finest performance I've ever seen!

_____

8. Believe it or not I danced and twirled all the way home.

_____

Name _____ Date _____

Commas for Introductory Phrases

When a sentence begins with an introductory phrase, use a comma to set off the phrase from the rest of the sentence.

In the first book of the trilogy, the explorers see something shocking.

Rewrite each sentence. Add a comma to set off the introductory phrase.

1. As a lover of science I found this research fascinating.

_____

2. Once I am inside the laboratory I put on my safety goggles.

_____

3. Every afternoon light shines through the western windows.

_____

4. Because of the strong sunlight I sometimes lower the window shades.

_____

5. Despite some frightening scenes horror novels appeal to me.

_____

6. With so much to do this week I cannot visit the library.

_____

Commas

Within a sentence, commas are used to set off introductory words or phrases, separate words in a series or list, and divide two independent clauses joined by a coordinating conjunction such as **and** or **but**.

In fact, I saw Ravi, Joaquin, and Amy at recess, but my other friends were not there.

For each sentence, write the element that the comma or commas sets off: *introductory phrase*, *words in a series*, or *two independent clauses*.

1. My family went to the zoo, and I was eager to see the reptiles.

_____

2. Prior to this visit, we had never been to the zoo.

_____

3. First we saw jaguars, cheetahs, and apes.

_____

4. My favorite animal was the giraffe, but my sister's favorite was the baby hippo.

_____

5. We were excited to see the exhibits, visit the gift shop, and buy some trinkets.

_____

6. After such a fun day, we asked if we could visit the aquarium next year.

_____

Rewrite each sentence. Add commas where needed.

7. I saw roses daffodils and daisies but I couldn't decide which ones to buy.

_____

8. After staying up late I was really tired for the entire day.

_____

Name _____ Date _____

Commas

Within a sentence, commas are used to set off introductory words or phrases and to separate three or more items listed in a series. A comma is often used to separate two independent clauses joined by **and**, **but**, or **so** in a compound sentence.

All week, we planted bulbs, so we will have daffodils, tulips, and irises next spring.

Add the necessary commas to each sentence.

1. In the morning Lily woke at sunrise.

2. She was going to the beach but first she needed to prepare.

3. She packed sunscreen sandwiches and a striped beach umbrella.

4. At first she couldn't find anywhere to spread out her beach towels.

5. She found a spot right by the lifeguard tower and it was perfect.

6. She watched the seagulls swoop soar and dive into the ocean to catch a fish.

Rewrite each sentence. Add commas where needed.

7. In the late afternoon a nearby family packed up their blanket towels and umbrella but there was no food left to take home.

_____

_____

8. After a short wait the bus came and Sasha Nate and I got on with our stuff.

_____

Name _____ Date _____

Commas

> Within a sentence, commas are used to set off introductory words or phrases, separate words in a series or list, and divide two independent clauses joined by a coordinating conjunction such as **and** or **but**.
>
> At the store, he bought fruit, eggs, and cheese, but he forgot to get milk.

Add commas to each sentence. Then determine whether the comma or commas set off an introductory phrase, words in a series, two independent clauses, or a combination of the three. Write _I_ for introductory phrase, _S_ for series, _C_ for compound sentence.

1. I studied algebra geometry and measurement. _____

2. In the beginning Jason liked Ms. Wilson's chemistry class best. _____

3. Later on he found that he also enjoyed history but he still liked chemistry more. _____ _____

4. The bell rang at 2:15 p.m. and we went outside to play volleyball. _____

5. At first Chris and I scored the most points, but then Micah and Joelle outscored us. _____ _____

6. It was fun so Joelle Micah and Chris decided to play every week. _____ _____

7. I enjoy the time I spend with my mom dad and brothers. _____

8. When I got home I took a long bath. _____

Commas

Within a sentence, commas are used to set off introductory words or phrases, separate words in a series or list, and divide two independent clauses joined by a coordinating conjunction such as **and** or **but**.

Wow, that was such an exciting adventure movie!
I have to buy lemons, limes, sugar, and a pitcher.
It started to rain, but Sergio had his umbrella.

Rewrite each sentence. Add commas where needed.

1. Earlier the doorbell rang.

_____

2. Nicole Marcus and Tommy had arrived.

_____

3. Tommy wanted to do homework but Nicole wanted to watch funny videos.

_____

4. We took out our textbooks our notes and our pencils.

_____

5. The next thing we knew our work was done and we could watch some videos.

_____

6. Marcus recommended his favorites and we spent the rest of the afternoon laughing.

_____

Commas

Use commas to separate three or more items in a series, and before the conjunction **and** or **or** in a series.
   I can't decide between **a veggie burger, sushi, or soup** for lunch.
   Please buy **a bag of potatoes, a box of tea, and a gallon of milk.**
   My uncle ran in the **2009, 2010, 2011, and 2013** Boston marathons.

Rewrite each sentence. Add commas where needed.

1. We will serve fried chicken macaroni salad and juice at the birthday party.

_____

2. We decorated the party room on Thursday Friday and Saturday.

_____

3. We have red blue and yellow streamers.

_____

4. Dozens of balloons were purchased inflated and tied up by noon on Saturday.

_____

5. We could smell the aroma of the food cooking from the living room the dining room and the hallway.

_____

_____

6. Decorations friends and delicious food make parties fun!

_____

7. The guests gathered in the living room the kitchen and the yard.

_____

Conquer Grammar • Grade 5 • © Newmark Learning, LLC

Commas in Dialogue

If the speaker is identified before the dialogue, place a comma after the speaker's tag. If the speaker is introduced after the dialogue, place a comma inside the final quotation mark. Drop the comma, however, if the quote ends in a question mark or an exclamation point.

Soraya asked, "Do you see the bus?"

"I don't see it coming," answered Alex.

Rewrite each sentence. Add commas where needed.

1. Julio asked "Dad, can Byron and I go to a movie?"

_____

2. Dad asked "Have you put away the dishes?"

_____

3. "I put everything away" answered Julio.

_____

4. Dad said "That's great! Have fun."

_____

5. "Thanks! I'll let you know how I liked it" said Julio.

_____

6. Byron said "I'll buy the popcorn!"

_____

7. "Don't have too much junk food" Mom said.

_____

8. "We won't, we promise" Julio said.

_____

Commas in Dialogue

Purpose of Comma in Dialogue	Example
to indicate direct address	"Spence, do you want to walk?"
to set off introductory words like **yes** or **no**	"No, my science project is too fragile."
to set off a tag question	"We will walk home, won't we?"

Rewrite each sentence. Add commas where needed.

1. "Are you trying out for choir Jeannie?" asked Carmela.

_____

2. "Yes here is the song I want to sing" she said.

_____

3. Carmela said "Oh that's the same song I planned to sing!"

_____

4. Jeannie said "We can both sing it can't we?"

_____

5. "I have an idea. Let's sing it as a duet" said Jeannie.

_____

6. Carmela replied "Yes that would be memorable right?"

_____

7. "Exactly that is a good compromise," Jeannie said.

_____

8. "I am excited to sing with you Jeannie!" Carmela replied.

_____

Commas in Dialogue

Purpose of Comma in Dialogue	Example
to set off the speaker's tag: if the speaker is identified before the dialogue, place a comma after the speaker's tag.	**Simone said,** "I don't see the train."
to set off the speaker's tag: if the speaker is identified after the dialogue, place a comma inside the final quotation mark.	"I don't see it either**,"** **replied Olivia.**
to indicate direct address	Simone said, "**Olivia,** I think you won!"
to set off introductory words like **yes** or **no**	Olivia said, "**No,** I didn't!"
to set off a tag question	"We will walk home, **won't we?**"

Rewrite each sentence. Add commas where needed.

1. Elias asked his sister "Which park should we go to Ava?"

_____

2. Ava said "Let's go to the one with the pool okay?"

_____

3. Elias said "No I think that one is too far."

_____

4. "Well the one with the bike trail is closer isn't it?" Ava said.

_____

5. "Yep and it's a perfect day for riding bikes" said Elias.

_____

6. Ava said "Wow this is going to be a fun day!"

_____

7. Elias said "Yes I am so excited!"

_____

8. Ava asked her brother "Should we leave now Elias?"

_____

Name _____ Date _____

Commas in Dialogue

Purpose of Comma in Dialogue	Example
to set off the speaker's tag: if the speaker is identified before the dialogue, place a comma after the speaker's tag.	**Gisele said,** "Cory, let's get lunch, okay?"
to set off the speaker's tag: if the speaker is identified after the dialogue, place a comma inside the final quotation mark.	"I liked the movie**,"** **George said.**
to indicate direct address	Taylor asked, **"Mary,** how are you?"
to set off introductory words like **yes** or **no**	Beth said, **"Yes,** of course I will come with you."
to set off a tag question	"We will go to the store, **won't we?"**

Rewrite each sentence. Add commas where needed.

1. Jody asked "What time do we have to be at the event?"

_____

2. Scott said, "We should be there by noon Jody."

_____

3. Jody asked "Should we leave in an hour?"

_____

4. "Yes I'll go gather my things," Scott answered.

_____

5. "Sharee will be at the event won't she?" Scott asked.

_____

56

Conquer Grammar • Grade 5 • © Newmark Learning, LLC

Punctuate Quotations

A quotation is the exact words spoken by a real person. Use quotation marks to set off the speaker's exact words. If the person being quoted is identified first, place a comma before the first quotation mark. If the person being quoted is identified after the quote, place a comma inside the final quotation mark. Place periods inside quotation marks. If the quote itself ends in a question mark or an exclamation point, place the punctuation inside the final quotation mark and drop the comma. Always capitalize the first word in the quotation marks. If the quote is interrupted, do not capitalize the first word in the continuation.

President Roosevelt said, "The only thing we have to fear is fear itself."

Each sentence below contains a quote. Rewrite each sentence with proper punctuation and capitalization.

1. My violin teacher used to say practice makes perfect.

_____

2. Mark Twain once said the secret to getting ahead is getting started.

_____

3. Mother always claims the early bird catches the worm.

_____

4. Shakespeare once wrote better three hours too soon than a minute too late.

_____

5. From the sidelines, our coach shouts you can do it!

_____

6. Our teacher always states remember to turn in your homework.

_____

Punctuation for Effect

Use an exclamation point at the end of a statement that shows strong emotion, such as excitement, surprise, happiness, or fear. Use a period at the end of a statement that does not show strong emotion.

> I can't believe that I won first prize!
> We are going to the pool today.

Circle whether each sentence shows strong emotion or not.
Then write the correct end punctuation.

1. I'm thrilled that we got a puppy yesterday _____

strong emotion   not strong emotion

2. It is my job to feed him in the morning _____

strong emotion   not strong emotion

3. I was surprised when he licked my face _____

strong emotion   not strong emotion

4. His tail wagged as I wiped my face clean _____

strong emotion   not strong emotion

5. Never in my life have I seen a happier dog _____

strong emotion   not strong emotion

6. After a family vote, we named him Julius _____

strong emotion   not strong emotion

Punctuation for Effect

Use an exclamation point at the end of a statement that shows strong emotion, such as excitement, surprise, happiness, or fear. Use a period at the end of a statement that does not show strong emotion.

I can't wait to go to the beach**!**
I entered a pie in the baking contest**.**

**Circle whether each sentence shows strong emotion or not.
Then write the correct end punctuation.**

1. We got so much rain yesterday _____

strong emotion   not strong emotion

2. Ramona walked down the block _____

strong emotion   not strong emotion

3. She couldn't believe she got caught in the rain _____

strong emotion   not strong emotion

4. I brought my umbrella _____

strong emotion   not strong emotion

5. I couldn't believe my eyes _____

strong emotion   not strong emotion

6. Suddenly, a flash of lightning lit the sky _____

strong emotion   not strong emotion

Capitalize Proper Nouns

A proper noun names a specific person, place, or thing. Each main word of a proper noun should begin with a capital letter. The titles and names of people, the days of the week and the months of the year, and specific holidays and names of geographic places are proper nouns.

On **Sunday, Marla** will visit the **Museum of Fine Art**.
Last **June**, the **Jones** family went to a beach in **New Jersey**.

Circle the proper nouns that should be capitalized. Then rewrite the sentence correctly. Underline any book titles.

1. Every wednesday, I go to central library after school.

   _____

2. One of the librarians is named alicia morgan.

   _____

3. Miss morgan told me about a book sale next saturday afternoon.

   _____

4. Maybe I will find a book by jerry spinelli, my favorite author.

   _____

5. My older brother wayne likes robinson crusoe and other adventure classics.

   _____

6. Once we buy our books, we will go to finley park to read them

   _____

Capitalization in Dialogue

Quotation marks set off a speaker's exact words. Always capitalize the first word in the quotation marks. If the dialogue is interrupted, do not capitalize the first word in the continuation of the dialogue.

"**L**et's meet on the lower field today," said my coach.

Rewrite each sentence with correct capitalization.

1. Mr. Jefferson announced, "your rough drafts are due tomorrow."

_____

2. "what is the topic of your research paper?" asked Ellie.

_____

3. "the topic I chose is Rome," I said. "my grandfather lives there."

_____

4. Ellie wondered, "have you ever been there for a visit?"

_____

5. "yes, but it's been a long time since I last visited," I answered.

_____

6. "there are so many ancient ruins there," I shared. "it's hard to miss them."

_____

Capitalization and Punctuation in Titles

Capitalize the first word and each additional main word of a book or song title. Unless it is the first word of the title, do not capitalize **a**, **an**, and **the**, or most short prepositions, such as **at**, **in**, **by**, **for**, **of**, and **to**. Always underline a book, movie, or magazine title and place an article, poem, song, or story title in quotation marks.

Book title: I just read <u>Maniac Magee</u>.
Poem title: "A Spring Day" is a beautiful poem.

Underline or add quotation marks for the title in each sentence.
Then rewrite the sentence with correct punctuation and capitalization
for the title.

1. I borrowed big cats of south america from the library.

   _____

2. Have you seen my book, chasing vermeer?

   _____

3. The article, island of the blue dolphins, is very informative

   _____

4. The author of survival in antarctica visited our school

   _____

5. I bought intermediate camping tips to take on our trip.

   _____

Name _____ Date _____

Capitalization and Punctuation in Titles

Capitalize the first word and each additional main word of a book or song title. Unless it is the first or last word of the title, do not capitalize **a**, **an**, and **the**, or most short prepositions, such as **at**, **in**, **by**, **for**, **of**, and **to**. Always underline a book, movie, or magazine title and place an article, poem, song, or story title in quotation marks.

> **Book title:** <u>The Lightning Thief</u>
> **Song title:** "America the Beautiful"

Rewrite each sentence with correct capitalization. Be sure to underline book titles and put quotation marks around song titles.

1. I just finished reading the best way to train a parrot.

_____

2. I read a book called cooking and science and found out how the topics are similar.

_____

3. Our country's national anthem is called the star-spangled banner.

_____

4. I just bought the book, bridge to terabithia.

_____

5. The first song I can remember singing is mary had a little lamb.

_____

6. My mother's favorite mystery novel is a study in scarlet.

_____

Temporal Words

Temporal words and phrases signal the order in which events occur. They make the timing of events clear.

Evan **first** went to the library and **then** he went home.
Yvonne went to the store **after** studying **for several hours**.

Underline the temporal word or phrase in each sentence.

1. The third time we went to the lake was the best.

2. What did we do two months ago?

3. An hour after we had lunch, we went back to the lake.

4. The village near the lake was established 100 years ago.

5. A year from now, I hope we will all meet here again.

6. We will be so happy when our friends arrive in a couple of hours.

7. I will set up for the picnic before they arrive.

8. I hope to be done one hour from now.

Rewrite each sentence. Add a temporal word or phrase to make the timing of events clear.

9. Do you want to walk the dog _____?

_____

10. I have to go to the doctor _____, but I can join you before dinner.

_____

_____

Name _____ Date _____

Temporal Words

> Temporal words and phrases signal the order in which events occur. They make the timing of events clear.
>
> I'm looking forward to seeing the movie **over the weekend**.
> I hope we'll stop for pizza **after** the movie.
> Did you know that it took **more than two years** to make this movie?

Underline the temporal words in each sentence.

1. We bought a special kite last week.

2. It took us many days to learn how to fly it.

3. After a short time, we were able to fly the kite successfully.

4. My sister and I kept that beautiful kite in the air for a while.

5. We read that the Chinese invented kites more than 2,000 years ago!

Rewrite each sentence. Add a temporal word or phrase to make the timing of events clear.

6. Aaron wanted to go swimming _____.

_____

7. Can you come to my graduation party _____?

_____

Temporal Words

Temporal words and phrases signal the order in which events occur. They make the timing of events clear.

Can we go to the dog park **after school**?

I saw a great movie **last Saturday**.

Janie's parents moved to this country **fifteen years ago**.

Identify the temporal words or phrases in each sentence and write them on the line.

1. We went to a restaurant tonight after Mom got home. _____

2. At first, we were going to drive, but then we decided to bike. _____

3. Ten minutes later, we arrived at our destination. _____

4. I ordered a bowl of soup first, and next I ordered a burger. _____

5. Our meals were on the table in just a few minutes. _____

6. I would really like to eat there again on Friday night. _____

Rewrite each sentence. Add a temporal word or phrase to make the timing of events clear.

7. Will you go to the amusement park _____?

_____

8. We had a much worse hurricane _____.

_____

Sentence Fragments

A sentence fragment is an incomplete sentence that does not express a complete thought. It is missing a subject, a verb, or both. To correct a fragment, add the missing subject or verb.

Fragment: Crept along the shore.
Corrected: A **hermit crab** crept along the shore.
Fragment: The bird in the wind.
Corrected: The bird **soared** in the wind.

Circle whether the fragment is missing a subject or a verb. Rewrite the fragment as a complete sentence using one of the phrases below the fragment.

1. Planted lots of apple trees. (missing a subject, missing a verb)

Farmer Brown   spent

_____

2. She the orchard with great care. (missing a subject, missing a verb)

Julie   tended

_____

3. Some pumpkins from the farm fifty pounds! (missing a subject, missing a verb)

Milly   weighed

_____

4. Awarded Farmer Brown a blue ribbon. (missing a subject, missing a verb)

the judges   had

_____

5. Will she grow next season? (missing a subject, missing a verb)

what   got

_____

Name _____ Date _____

Sentence Fragments

A sentence fragment is an incomplete sentence that does not express a complete thought. It is missing a subject, a verb, or both. To correct a fragment, add the missing subject or verb.

Fragment: The cat its tail happily.
Complete sentence: The cat **wagged** its tail happily.
Fragment: Meowed when I filled its food dish.
Complete sentence: The cat meowed when I filled its food dish.

Circle whether the sentence is missing a subject or a verb. Then rewrite the sentence with a subject or verb that best completes the sentence.

1. I strawberry ice cream.   subject   verb

_____

2. Contains many diagrams.   subject   verb

_____

3. Will have a math test next week.   subject   verb

_____

4. That birthday card very thoughtful.   subject   verb

_____

5. Why did leave?   subject   verb

_____

6. Who the person laughing?   subject   verb

_____

Name _____ Date _____

Run-On Sentences

A run-on sentence contains two or more complete thoughts. One way to correct a run-on sentence is to separate it into two or more sentences, each with a subject and a verb. Another way is to add a comma between the complete thoughts and a coordinating conjunction such as **and**, **but**, **or**, or **so**.

Run-on: The cat was orange and had white stripes it looked at its owner as it went to drink milk.

Corrected: The cat was orange and had white stripes. **It** looked at its owner as it went to drink milk.

Rewrite each run-on sentence as two complete sentences.

1. Here is a book that I would love to read it is about the wilderness.

_____

2. The first picture is of two bears in a river the water looks very cold!

_____

3. This chapter is about rivers some are in the West, while others are in the East.

_____

4. In the next chapter, there is a picture of a bear its fur is shiny and thick.

_____

5. If I were a bear, I would climb up the tree quickly the branches look sturdy.

_____

6. One page shows people hiking their packs look very heavy.

_____

Name _____ Date _____

Run-On Sentences

A run-on sentence contains two or more complete thoughts. One way to correct a run-on sentence is to separate it into two or more sentences, each with a subject and a verb. Another way is to add a comma between the complete thoughts and a coordinating conjunction such as **and**, **but**, **or**, or **so**.

Run-on: The class read "The Legend of Sleepy Hollow" the students decided to perform it as reader's theater.

Corrected: The class read "The Legend of Sleepy Hollow**." T**he students decided to perform it as reader's theater.

Rewrite each run-on sentence as two complete sentences.

1. We're sorry we arrived to your house late we were stuck in traffic.

_____

2. The championship track meet was on all the runners ran so fast!

_____

3. Should I tell you the name of the book I think you would really like it?

_____

4. I wrote down the recipe while we were watching the cooking show everything looked delicious and easy to make.

_____

_____

5. Ask your mom if you can come over we can study for our test.

_____

6. We'll make a good breakfast we just have to pick up a dozen eggs.

_____

Run-On Sentences

A run-on sentence contains two or more complete thoughts. One way to correct a run-on sentence is to separate it into two or more sentences, each with a subject and a verb. Another way is to add a comma between the complete thoughts and a coordinating conjunction such as **and**, **but**, **or**, or **so**.

Run-on: My dad prepared supper we ate it in an hour and then had dessert that I liked but my sister didn't because it was crunchy.

Corrected: My dad prepared supper. **W**e ate it in an hour and then had dessert. **I** liked the dessert**, b**ut my sister didn't because it was crunchy.

Rewrite each run-on sentence as two or more complete sentences.

1. My brothers and I will go hiking this weekend and our father will take us to a local trail.

_____

_____

2. We need water to drink hydration is important when exercising.

_____

3. I have hiked only once before hiking is very exciting.

_____

4. The trail is three miles and when we are hiking up the hill, we will be tired but when we go down, it should be easier.

_____

_____

5. The sun is shining brightly now maybe later it will be cloudy, which will make the day cooler.

_____

_____

Sentence Fragments and Run-On Sentences

A sentence fragment does not express a complete thought. It is missing a subject, a verb, or both. To correct a fragment, add the missing subject or verb. A run-on sentence consists of two or more complete thoughts. One way to correct a run-on sentence is to divide it into two or more complete sentences.

Fragment: A flock of birds in a tree.
Corrected: We saw a flock of birds in a tree.

Run-on: They flew off when the wind shook the tree leaves fell down on us as we stood there watching the birds.
Corrected: They flew off when the wind shook the tree. Leaves fell down on us as we stood there watching the birds.

Determine whether each sentence is a run-on sentence or a fragment. Write the answer on the line.

1. The boy with a toy truck. _____

2. Sipped from the straw. _____

3. I have a younger sister who is two and she is great I love watching her learn to talk. _____

4. The first word she said was "ball" and my father was so excited he whooped with laughter and so did I. _____

Rewrite each run-on sentence as two or more complete sentences.

5. I squealed and said the word again everyone began to laugh.

_____

6. I asked my father what my first word was and it was the very same word my sister had said and I was amazed!

_____

_____

Combine Sentences

Use the conjunction **and** or **or** to join the subjects (if the predicate appears in both sentences) or predicates (if the subject appears in both sentences) of two sentences.

Blair played on the tennis team. Jane played on the tennis team.
Blair **and** Jane played on the tennis team.

Combine each pair of sentences with the conjunction *and* or *or*.
Write the sentence on the line.

1. Strawberries are very nutritious. Blueberries are very nutritious.

_____

2. The Bears could win the tournament. The Lions could win the tournament.

_____

3. My friend Maurice rode the roller coaster. My friend Tommy rode the roller coaster.

_____

4. Anna biked to the beach. Manuel biked to the beach.

_____

5. My mother likes to sing. I like to sing.

_____

6. The balloons were for the party. The cake was for the party.

_____

7. My dad might tell a scary ghost story. Dad's brother might tell a scary ghost story.

_____

Combine Sentences

Use the conjunction **and** or **or** to join the subjects (if the predicate appears in both sentences) or predicates (if the subject appears in both sentences) of two sentences.

The baby smiled widely. The baby giggled loudly.
The baby smiled widely **and** giggled loudly.

Combine each pair of sentences with the conjunction *and* or *or*.
Write the sentence on the line.

1. The storm rained out the softball game. The storm ruined the picnic.

_____

2. I might stay up late. I might go to bed early.

_____

3. I bike on Saturdays. I swim on Sundays.

_____

4. The cat naps on the bed. The cat dozes in a patch of sun.

_____

5. The cup fell off the counter. The cup broke.

_____

6. The flight could be delayed one hour. The flight could be delayed two hours.

_____

7. According to Bob, it should be hot today. It should be humid today.

_____

Name _____ Date _____

Compound Sentences

Use a comma and a coordinating conjunction such as **and**, **or**, **but**, **for**, **nor**, **so**, and **yet** to combine two sentences to make a compound sentence.

It was very hot**, so** it was difficult to run the cross-country workout.

**Combine each pair of sentences to form a compound sentence.
Use a comma and the correct coordinating conjunction.**

1. Miguel twisted his ankle. He skinned his elbow, too.

_____

2. He wanted to play in the game. His coach advised against it.

_____

3. Miguel wanted to disregard the advice. He actually agreed with it.

_____

4. Should he stay for the game? Should he go home instead?

_____

5. Miguel watched from the bench. His coach smiled in approval.

_____

6. Miguel wanted to participate. He cheered the loudest for his team.

_____

Complex Sentences

A complex sentence consists of an independent clause joined with a dependent clause by a subordinate conjunction. Subordinate conjunctions include **although**, **since**, **because**, **until**, **while**, **that**, **when**, and **where**. If the conjunction the sentence, place a comma between the clauses.

I did my homework in the library **until** it closed.
Although I worked steadily**,** I didn't finish the assignments.

Draw one line under the independent clause. Draw two lines under the dependent clause.

1. The fawn stayed close to the herd because there was a wolf nearby.

2. The herd was on high alert while the wolf remained.

3. The wolf gave up in exasperation since he could not approach the fawn.

4. Although the herd was nervous, it did not scatter.

Combine the two sentences to form a complex sentence. Use a subordinate conjunction from the box above.

5. Ants work together for survival. They are social insects.

_____

6. Ants are tiny. They are very strong.

_____

7. They follow the other ants in a line. This helps the ants find food efficiently.

_____

Name _____ Date _____

Complex Sentences

A complex sentence consists of an independent clause joined with a dependent clause by a subordinate conjunction. Subordinate conjunctions include **although**, **since**, **because**, **until**, **while**, **that**, **when**, and **where**. If the conjunction begins the sentence, place a comma between the clauses.

I shopped for clothes at the mall. It closed.
I shopped for clothes at the mall **until** it closed.

I had money to spend. I didn't buy anything.
Although I had money to spend, I didn't buy anything.

Combine the two sentences to form a complex sentence.
Use a subordinate conjunction from the box above.

1. The author is coming out with a collection of short stories. I am not sure if I want to buy a copy.

_____

_____

2. I had my rain boots. My feet and socks stayed dry.

_____

3. The weather is cold. I will wear this sweater.

_____

4. I won't go in the ocean. The water is cold and the waves are big.

_____

5. The wind blew the trees. I walked through the park.

_____

Expand, Combine, or Reduce Sentences

Reduce sentences by deleting unnecessary words and phrases.

Expand sentences by adding important descriptive information.

Combine two sentences into one sentence.

Reduce: When I was ten years old ~~or maybe ten and a half~~, I learned to ski.

Expand: The traffic was terrible **on the highway**.

Combine: The traffic was slow, **but** we arrived in time.

Allie wasn't in school today **because** she was ill.

Write whether the second sentence expands, combines, or reduces the first sentence or sentences.

1. a. The mother of my friend whom I knew from school saw to me first.

   b. My school friend's mother saw to me first.

   _____

2. a. It was a warm day. It was a windy day, too.

   b. It was a warm day, and it was windy, too.

   _____

3. a. She liked how the petals of the flower that were wet shone in the sun.

   b. She liked how the flower's wet petals shone in the sun.

   _____

4. a. My aunt is loving.

   b. My aunt, who's in the kitchen, is loving.

   _____

5. a. I'm glad that she made so many ice pops.

   b. I'm glad that she made so many ice pops in this heat.

   _____

Conquer Grammar • Grade 5 • © Newmark Learning, LLC

Expand, Combine, or Reduce Sentences

Reduce sentences by deleting unnecessary words and phrases.
Expand sentences by adding important descriptive information.
Combine two sentences into one sentence.

Reduce: We drove ~~and I sat in the back seat~~ on curvy mountain roads.

Expand: I went to the baseball game **that was the winning game of the World Series!**

Combine: Traffic was heavy**, but** we still got there before the game started.

Rewrite each pair of sentences. Follow the instructions in the parentheses ( ) to expand, combine, or reduce the sentences.

1. The jaguar at the zoo had sleek fur. It had intense eyes.   (combine)

_____

2. My friend, who is named Clara just like her mother, sketched the gorillas. (reduce)

_____

3. The guide said not to take flash photos.   (expand)

_____

4. Nora waved her hands and waved her fingers at the lion cub.   (reduce)

_____

5. The cub looked startled.   (expand)

_____

6. The guide said that the cub was very young. It likes to be near its mother. (combine)

_____

Name _____ Date _____

Dictionaries

Use a dictionary to check the spelling, pronunciation, part of speech, and meaning of a word. Words in a dictionary are listed in alphabetical order, from **a** to **z**. Print dictionaries have two guide words on every page. The first guide word represents the first word on the page. The second guide word represents the last word on the page.

Guide words: gadget • **gas**p
Included on the page: game
Not included: gather

For each pair of guide words, write *yes* or *no* to answer the question.

1. adamant   •   advancement

Is the word **address** on this page? _____

2. chairman   •   chowder

Is the word **chute** on this page? _____

3. facility   •   fathom

Is the word **fastener** on this page? _____

4. lagoon   •   lava

Is the word **laughter** on this page? _____

5. necessary   •   neighbor

Is the word **nervous** on this page? _____

6. pail   •   partner

Is the word **panel** on this page? _____

7. dog   •   domestic

Is the word **donate** on this page? _____

8. service   •   setter

Is the word **session** on this page? _____

Name _____ Date _____

Dictionaries

Use a dictionary to check the spelling, pronunciation, part of speech, and meaning of a word. Words in a dictionary are listed in alphabetical order, from **a** to **z**. Print dictionaries have two guide words on every page. The first guide word represents the first word on the page. The second guide word represents the last word on the page.

Guide words: sunshine • **sup**per

Included on the page: super

Not included: support

For each pair of guide words, write *yes* **or** *no* **to answer the question.**

1. charm   •   check

   Is the word **chatter** on this page? _____

2. distaste   •   dive

   Is the word **district** on this page? _____

3. official   •   old

   Is the word **optical** on this page? _____

4. spread   •   spruce

   Is the word **sprinkle** on this page? _____

5. fair   •   fall

   Is the word **fare** on this page? _____

6. errand   •   establish

   Is the word **essay** on this page? _____

7. vary   •   veil

   Is the word **vast** on this page? _____

8. admit   •   adult

   Is the word **advance** on this page? _____

Homophones

Homophones are words that sound the same but have different spellings and meanings. Some examples include **there/their/they're**, **through/threw**, and **rap/wrap**.

The pitcher **threw** the ball and it soared **through** the air.

Circle the two words that sound the same in each sentence.
Then write the word that matches the definition.

1. If you have a cut on your heel, a bandage will help you heal quicker.
   Improve is another word for _____.

2. The principal makes it a principle to treat all of the students kindly and fairly.   **Chief** is another word for _____.

3. Students are not allowed to talk aloud without raising their hand and being called on.   **Permitted** is another word for _____.

4. The tourists heard that the herd of moose had moved to another area in the park.   **Group** is another word for _____.

5. Whether rain or shine, the weather won't stop us from weeding the garden.
   Either is another word for _____.

6. The seller kept extra supplies in the cellar of the shop.
   Basement is another word for _____.

7. The mess at the site of the demolished building was an unpleasant sight.
   Location is another word for _____.

8. A dentist should treat all her patients with patience.
   Calmness is another word for _____.

Name _____ Date _____

Homophones

Homophones are words that sound the same but have different spellings and meanings. Some examples include **peace/piece**, **flu/flew**, **wear/where**, and **new/knew**.

Where did I leave the scarf I want to **wear**?

Circle the two words that sound the same in each sentence.
Then write the word that matches the definition.

1. Val is going to try out for the school play, and I will, too.

Also is another word for _____.

2. I see that they're at the kitchen eating their dinner.

The word _____ is a contraction.

3. My brother sometimes gets bored when we play a board game.

Disinterested is another word for _____.

4. It's fun to watch the kitten chase its toy.

The word _____ is a possessive pronoun.

5. Salvatore felt weak for a whole week after being sick.

The opposite of **strong** is _____.

6. Michelle threw the basketball through the hoop and won the game.

Tossed is another word for _____.

7. Gerrold knew that the new action movie would be good.

If you were aware of it, you _____.

Name _____ Date _____

Homophones

Homophones are words that sound the same but have different spellings and meanings. Some examples include **two/too/to**, **here/hear**, **deer/dear**, and **course/coarse**.

  Incorrect: Those to games go in **hear**, **to**.
  Correct: Those **two** games go in **here**, **too**.

Circle the correct word in the parentheses ( ) to complete each sentence. Then write the correct word for each definition.

1. The captain changed the (coarse, course) of the ship to avoid the storm.

  It means **direction**. _____

  It means **rough**. _____

2. We went to our local post office to (male, mail) our packages.

  It means a **man** or **boy**. _____

  It means "send by post." _____

3. Sometimes she gets (board, bored) with historical fiction.

  It means **uninterested**. _____

  It is a piece of wood. _____

4. Thanks, we received the two samples you (sent, cent).

  It is a unit of money. _____

  It means "moved something from one place to another."_____

5. We froze in our tracks, so that we wouldn't scare the (dear, deer) off.

  It is a hoofed animal. _____

  It is a greeting in a letter. _____

Name _____ Date _____

Homophones

Homophones are words that sound the same but have different spellings and meanings. Some examples include **heard/herd** and **waist/waste**.

I **heard** from the farmhand that the **herd** was misbehaving.

Circle the incorrect word or words in each sentence. Then write the homophone of the word to make the sentence correct.

1. I'll get to my chores write away. _____

2. In exactly too seconds, I'll start working. _____

3. I no you herd me laughing before, but I'm ready to work now.

_____   _____

4. If I eight sum popcorn first, I might be more motivated. _____

_____

5. Theirs no need to frown. I won't waist any more time. _____

_____

6. I am sure that I'll be threw in an our. _____ _____

7. I can't weight to bee finished! _____ _____

8. Tyler is deciding weather to help me the hole day. _____

_____

Homophones

Homophones are words that sound the same but have different spellings and meanings. Some examples of homophones include contractions and possessive pronouns like the following: **they're/their**, **it's/its**, **you're/your**, **who's/whose**.

Contraction	Possessive Pronoun
they're (they are)	their
it's (it is)	its
you're (you are)	your
who's (who is)	whose

Write the contraction for the words in the parentheses ( ) and its homophone on the correct line to complete each sentence.

1. _____ going to visit _____ relatives for Thanksgiving. (they are)

2. Please lend me _____ scooter if _____ not going to use it. (you are)

3. _____ important to keep our puppy on _____ leash as we walk. (it is)

4. Dad told me, "I know _____ going to ace _____ test today!" (you are)

5. _____ fun to watch our dog chase _____ favorite ball. (it is)

6. _____ pencil is this on the floor? _____ missing a pencil? (who is)

7. My cat stares at _____ food dish to let me know _____ hungry or thirsty. (it is)

8. _____ jerseys indicate what team _____ on. (they are)

9. _____ book is that? _____ missing a book? (who is)

Informal and Formal Language

Informal language has a casual tone and consists of incomplete sentences and slang. Use informal language in friendly pieces of writing, such as an e-mail or a letter to a friend. Formal language consists of complete sentences and standard grammar. Use formal language in an essay or a letter to the editor. Avoid using contractions in formal pieces of writing.

Informal	**Formal**
Hey, want to grab lunch?	I wish to extend an invitation for lunch at noon.
Lou shouted, "Dude! It's been like forever since I saw you last!"	Lou said, "Hello, I have not seen you in a long time."

Circle whether each sentence has formal or informal language.

1. Wanna go to the mall after school?

   formal   informal

2. I wish to file a complaint about the noise in our neighborhood.

   formal   informal

3. Julio rolled his eyes at me, and I cracked up!

   formal   informal

4. That guy was like, "Who, me?"

   formal   informal

5. I would be grateful if you could send me details about your summer camp.

   formal   informal

6. There is no way I'd ever see that scary movie.

   formal   informal

Interjections and Informal Speech

Writers use informal speech in dialogue to indicate character and setting. They also often incorporate interjections, or short exclamations, to show a character's emotions, such as surprise or shock, excitement or fear. A strong interjection should end in an exclamation point. A comma should follow a mild interjection.

"**Yikes,** it looks as if we're **in for** a **real bad** storm," the lifeguard said.

Underline the informal speech or interjection in each sentence.

1. "Where are you going?" he hollered.

2. "Whoa," he said. "You're skating real fast!"

3. "Ain't a problem!" she shouted back gleefully.

4. "She acts as if it weren't nothin'," he said. "But she should cool it."

5. She skated around the block and back. "Gosh, that was fun!" she said.

6. "You're fixin' for trouble," he said.

7. Another skater zipped by. "Wow! Look at how fast he's goin'. I'm gonna catch up with him," she said.

Conquer Grammar • Grade 5 • © Newmark Learning, LLC

Interjections and Informal Speech

Writers use informal speech in dialogue to indicate character and setting. They also often incorporate interjections, or short exclamations, to show a character's emotions, such as surprise or shock, excitement or fear. A strong interjection should end in an exclamation point. A comma should follow a mild interjection.

Stop! Don't leave home without your wallet!
Hmm, where did I put my sunglasses?

Circle the informal speech or interjection in each sentence.
Write _I_ for informal speech, _S_ for strong interjection,
and _M_ for mild interjection.

1. Oh, I didn't know you'd be shopping for gifts, too. _____

2. I'm super kidding about disliking shopping. _____

3. Yikes! These party decorations are hideous! _____

4. Well, do you like these gold and silver ones? _____

Rewrite each sentence with the interjection in the parentheses ( ).
Be sure to use the correct punctuation for the interjection.

5. The train is pulling into the station. (hurry)

_____

6. I won the tournament. (wow)

_____

7. This book is overdue, so I'll return it to the library tomorrow. (well)

_____

Name _____ Date _____

Interjections and Informal Speech

Writers use informal speech in dialogue to indicate character and setting. They also often incorporate interjections, or short exclamations, to show a character's emotions, such as surprise or shock, excitement or fear. A strong interjection should end in an exclamation point. A comma should follow a mild interjection.

Hey! I have **tons** of things to tell you.
Well, let's **hang out**.

Rewrite each sentence with an interjection. Choose from one of the following interjections: *Hurry, Stop, Wow, Hmm, Yum, Yikes, Yay*. Be sure to use the correct punctuation for the interjection.

1. That is the most awesome kite I've ever seen!

_____

2. Let's hustle, or we'll miss our flight!

_____

3. That ice cream was so delicious.

_____

4. I have so many chores to finish.

_____

5. I won the grand prize in the contest!

_____

6. I wonder where you left your keys.

_____

7. Don't skate on that ice! See the cracks?

_____

                              Conquer Grammar • Grade 5 • © Newmark Learning, LLC

Name _____ Date _____

Precise Language

Use precise words or phrases to convey ideas in a clear way. Precise language makes a piece of writing more interesting because the reader is able to visualize what is being described.

General

The horse **ran** across the field.

Precise

The horse **galloped** across the field.

For each sentence, circle the words in the parentheses ( ) that are precise. Then write the complete sentence on the line.

1. Mr. Hirano (walked, trudged) along with the (enormous, big) package.

_____

2. The child (howled, cried) when he lost his (toy, fuzzy bear).

_____

3. A cat will often (make a sound, hiss) to (warn, tell) others that its angry.

_____

4. The (bad, destructive) toddler (went, ripped) through the toy store.

_____

5. Bees (go, buzz) from plant to plant (looking for, seeking) pollen.

_____

Answer Key

Page 8

Name _____ Date _____

Proper Nouns

A common noun names a general person, place, or thing.
Proper nouns name specific people, places, or things.
Each main word in a proper noun should begin with a capital letter.

Common Noun	Proper Noun
girl	Darla Lopez
stadium	Yankee Stadium
ocean	Arctic Ocean

Use the chart below to sort and match each common and proper noun in the box. Write each proper noun with the correct capitalization.

country	august	jackie robinson	lake tahoe
himalayas	holiday	lake	memorial day
athlete	month	australia	mountain range

Common Nouns	Proper Nouns
country	Australia
mountain range	Himalayas
holiday	Memorial Day
lake	Lake Tahoe
athlete	Jackie Robinson
month	August

Page 9

Name _____ Date _____

Plural Nouns

A plural noun names more than one person, place, or thing. Add **s** to the end of most nouns to make them plural. Sometimes the plural has a different ending. For nouns ending in **x**, **z**, **s**, **sh**, or **ch**, add **es**. For nouns ending in a consonant and **y**, change the **y** to **i** and add **es**.

Singular Noun	Plural Noun
lesson	lessons
lunch	lunches
class	classes

Rewrite each sentence with the plural form of the noun in the parentheses ( ).

1. (Bus) bring many of us to school.
   Buses bring many of us to school.

2. Today, Mrs. Davis has arranged our (desk) in a big circle.
   Today, Mrs. Davis has arranged our desks in a big circle.

3. In the middle of the circle are several (box).
   In the middle of the circle are several boxes.

4. All of the (student) wonder what the special activity will be.
   All of the students wonder what the special activity will be.

Circle the correct plural noun or nouns to complete each sentence.

5. Our fathers use (axs, (axes)) to chop some wood for our campfire.

6. My friend and I are in charge of washing the ((dishes), dishs) after the meal.

7. We put up our (tentes, (tents)) and then look for colorful (birdes, (birds)) in the trees.

Page 10

Name _____ Date _____

Irregular Plural Nouns

The plural form of some nouns is irregular because there are no clear spelling rules to follow when forming the plural. Sometimes a noun's spelling doesn't change at all.

Singular Noun	Plural Noun
man	men
foot	feet
die	dice

Complete each sentence with the plural form of the noun in the parentheses ( ). If necessary, use a dictionary for help.

1. The dentist cleans my _teeth_ twice each year. (tooth)

2. My neighbors are _freshmen_ in high school. (freshman)

3. The farmer saw _mice_ in the barn. (mouse)

4. We played a board game that used a pair of _dice_ . (die)

5. Thirty-eight _children_ are on this field trip to the aquarium. (child)

6. Maybe we will see _geese_ swimming in the lake. (goose)

7. Several _women_ were riding bicycles in the park. (woman)

8. How many _people_ can the auditorium hold? (person)

Page 11

Name _____ Date _____

Possessive Nouns

A possessive noun tells who or what owns something.
Use **'s** to show possession for one person, place, or thing
  The **dog's** toy squeaked.

If the noun is plural and ends in an **s**, add an apostrophe **'** to show possession.
  The **girls'** dog ran around happily.

For many irregular plural nouns, add an apostrophe **'** followed by **s** to show possession.
  The **children's** grandparents went on a trip.

Circle the possessive noun in each sentence. Then write whether it is singular or plural on the line.

1. My (uncle's) car just pulled into the driveway. _singular_

2. It was a big surprise to win the (contest's) grand prize! _singular_

3. All of the (tourists') luggage arrived on the following flight. _plural_

4. Unfortunately, the (teams') jerseys were the same color. _plural_

5. The (trees') leaves had fallen all over the yard. _plural_

6. The (lion's) roar was a hard sound to miss. _singular_

Answer Key

Name _____ Date _____

Verb Tenses

Present tense verbs tell about something that is happening right now.
Past tense verbs tell about something that has already happened.
Future tense verbs tell about something that will happen at a later time.
Use the same verb tense to describe actions that happen at the same time.
Present: As it **starts** to rain, my dog **runs** into the house.
Past: When the rain **stopped**, she **ran** out again.
Future: We **will go** on a picnic tomorrow.

Write the verb in the parentheses ( ) that correctly completes the sentence.

1. When I showed up late, Mr. Turner ___wondered___ why. (wondered, wonders)

2. I shared that I ___had gone___ to the dentist the day before. (had gone, go)

3. Mr. Turner ___told___ me what the class was doing. (told, tells)

4. I ___joined___ the group that was working on the science project. (join, joined)

5. Joey's grandmother ___gave___ it to him to share with his class. (gives, gave)

6. The project isn't finished yet, but it ___will be___ tomorrow. (will be, is)

7. We are excited to see how it ___turns___ out. (turned, turns)

8. She handed in the test yesterday and ___did___ very well. (did, does)

9. We ___asked___ a question because we felt confused. (asked, asks)

10. The audience ___clapped___ after the band played the song. (clap, clapped)

12 | Conquer Grammar • Grade 5 • © Newmark Learning, LLC

Page 12

Name _____ Date _____

Verb Tenses

Present tense verbs tell about something that is happening right now.
Past tense verbs tell about something that has already happened.
Future tense verbs tell about something that will happen at a later time.
Use the same verb tense to describe actions that happen at the same time.
Present: When the orchestra **comes** onstage, the audience **claps**.
Past: When the orchestra **came** onstage, the audience **clapped**.
Future: I **will attend** the concert.

Write the verb in the parentheses ( ) that correctly completes the sentence.

1. I get stage fright every time I ___perform___ in a piano recital.
   (will perform, perform)

2. I worked really hard and ___memorized___ this piece perfectly.
   (memorize, memorized)

3. Calvin was clapping while Dad and Mia ___were shouting___ "Bravo!"
   (were shouting, are shouting)

4. By the time the performance was over, I ___had relaxed___ .
   (have relaxed, had relaxed)

5. Even after I had left the stage, the audience still ___applauded___ .
   (applauded, applaude)

6. I will continue taking lessons because I ___realize___ how much I enjoy
   playing the piano.
   (realize, will realize)

7. My teacher says that she ___will put on___ another recital next spring.
   (had put on, will put on)

Conquer Grammar • Grade 5 • © Newmark Learning, LLC | 13

Page 13

Name _____ Date _____

Shifts in Verb Tense

Present tense verbs tell about something that is happening right now.
Past tense verbs tell about something that has already happened.
Future tense verbs tell about something that will happen at a later time.
Change tenses to describe actions that happen at different times.
The puppies **played** all afternoon and **are** now fast asleep.

Write the tense of each underlined verb on the lines:
present, past, or *future.*

1. The clouds parted early, and now the sky is filled with stars. ___past___ ___present___

2. I ate my dinner inside, but now I stand under the stars. ___past___ ___present___

3. I brought my flashlight because I am a little afraid of the dark. ___past___ ___present___

4. The grass is dry, although it was raining earlier today. ___present___ ___past___

5. My mother said the stars are twinkling. ___past___ ___present___

6. I love being outdoors, but I will go in soon. ___present___ ___future___

7. I am fine now, but I will get hungry later. ___present___ ___future___

Circle the verb in the parentheses ( ) that correctly completes the sentence.

8. We played soccer in the heat, and now we (**are**, is) exhausted.

9. Today was very hot, but we hope tomorrow (**will be**, can) cooler for the big game.

10. I rode my skateboard earlier, and now I (are, **am**) home.

11. We finished our homework, so now we (go, **will go**) swimming.

12. I just started watching the movie, and I (**will finish**, finish) it tonight.

14 | Conquer Grammar • Grade 5 • © Newmark Learning, LLC

Page 14

Name _____ Date _____

Shifts in Verb Tense

Present tense verbs tell about something that is happening right now.
Past tense verbs tell about something that has already happened.
Future tense verbs tell about something that will happen at a later time.
Change tenses to describe actions that happen at different times.
The people who **arrived** this morning **are** still here.
When it **gets** dark, we **will go** home.

Underline the two verbs that shift tenses in each sentence.

1. The fire crackled loudly earlier, but now it just burns quietly.

2. We overcooked our marshmallows, but we will eat them anyway.

3. We have some pineapple juice left, although we consumed a lot of it already.

4. We will sing songs later that are camp favorites.

Rewrite each sentence with the correct form of the verb in the parentheses ( ).

5. Our cabin leader will tell us a story before we (go, went) to sleep.
   Our cabin leader will tell us a story before we go to sleep.

6. We request spooky stories even though they (scared, might scare) all of us.
   We requested spooky stories even though they might scare all of us.

7. I went to the deli to (buy, bought) some sandwiches.
   I went to the deli to buy some sandwiches.

8. When I get home, I will wash the tomatoes and (made, make) a salad.
   When I get home, I will wash the tomatoes and make a salad.

9. Yesterday, I (cooked, cook) spaghetti sauce that we (will use, use) tonight.
   Yesterday, I cooked spaghetti sauce that we will use tonight.

10. Rob went to the restaurant and (picks, will pick) up his take-out order.
    Rob went to the restaurant and will pick up his take-out order.

Conquer Grammar • Grade 5 • © Newmark Learning, LLC | 15

Page 15

Answer Key

Page 16

Shifts in Verb Tense

Present tense verbs tell about something that is happening right now.
Past tense verbs tell about something that has already happened.
Future tense verbs tell about something that will happen at a later time.
Change tenses to describe actions that happen at different times.
  The coaches **are** so surprised that we **lost** the game.
  Our team **will practice** more than we **did** before.

Rewrite each sentence with the correct form of the verb in the parentheses ( ).

1. I will play tag with my friends until it (gets, got) dark.

   I will play tag with my friends until it gets dark.

2. When I yell my dog's name, he (will come, came) running to me.

   When I yell my dog's name, he will come running to me.

3. It was overcast, and now it (is, was) raining.

   It was overcast, and now it is raining.

4. Because it is raining, we (go, will go) back home.

   Because it is raining, we will go back home.

5. My dog chased a squirrel, so she (is, was) worn out now.

   My dog chased a squirrel, so she is worn out now.

6. I ran too much, so now my shins (are hurting, were hurting).

   I ran too much, so now my shins are hurting.

7. We are extremely happy that the home team (wins, won).

   We are extremely happy that the home team won.

Page 16

Page 17

Shifts in Verb Tense

Present tense verbs tell about something that is happening right now.
Past tense verbs tell about something that has already happened.
Future tense verbs tell about something that will happen at a later time.
Change tenses to describe actions that happen at different times.
  The children **planted** seeds that **will grow** into flowers this spring.

Rewrite each sentence with the future tense of the verb in the parentheses ( ).

1. He is out for a walk, but soon he (run).

   He is out for a walk, but soon he will run.

2. After he runs around the block ten times, he (stop).

   After he runs around the block ten times, he will stop.

3. The exercise he gets from running (help) him concentrate.

   The exercise he gets from running will help him concentrate.

4. If I do extra chores, I (earn) more spending money.

   If I do extra chores, I will earn more spending money.

5. I (finish) washing dishes before I watch a movie.

   I will finish washing dishes before I watch movie.

Rewrite each sentence. Use the correct tense for each verb in the parentheses ( ).

6. I (work) hard today, so I (rest) well tonight.

   I worked hard today, so I will rest well tonight.

7. Tomorrow, Andre (practice) before he (play) at the piano recital.

   Tomorrow, Andre will practice before he plays at the piano recital.

Page 17

Page 18

Present Perfect Tense

The present perfect tense tells about an action that starts in the past and ends in the present. It can also tell about changes or experiences that happen over a period of time. The present perfect tense uses the helping verb **has** or **have** with the past participle of the main verb.
  Sun Yen **has played** soccer for three years.
  We **have played** on the same soccer team for all three years.

Rewrite each sentence with the present perfect tense of the verb in the parentheses ( ).

1. I (like) studying with Anna this semester.

   I have liked studying with Anna this semester.

2. I (walk) to school with Felix every day this week.

   I have walked to school with Felix every day this week.

3. Our class (perform) in the talent show every year.

   Our class has performed in the talent show every year.

4. Mr. Alvarez (coach) the chess club ever since I joined.

   Mr. Alvarez has coached the chess club ever since I joined.

5. I (love) Frank's banana bread for the last year.

   I have loved Frank's banana bread for the last year.

6. Beatrice (want) to become an author for a long time, and we (encourage) her.

   Beatrice has wanted to become an author for a long time, and we have encouraged her.

Page 18

Page 19

Present Perfect Tense

The present perfect tense tells about an action that starts in the past and ends in the present. It can also tell about changes or experiences that happen over a period of time. The present perfect tense uses the helping verb **has** or **have** with the past participle of a main verb.
  Rosaria **has loved** to garden all her life.
  Andy and Eddie **have played** the flute since last summer.

Rewrite each sentence with the perfect tense of the verb in the parentheses ( ).

1. I (help) my grandmother bake since I was very young.

   I have helped my grandmother bake since I was very young.

2. If your brother (finish) writing his story, may I read it?

   If your brother has finished his story, may I read it?

3. We (climb) to the peak of Mt. Charles twice.

   We have climbed to the peak of Mt. Charles twice.

4. Mark and Eduardo (attend) the same summer camp for two years in a row.

   Mark and Eduardo have attended the same summer camp for two years in a row.

5. Mr. Singh (travel) to Toronto several times.

   Mr. Singh has traveled to Toronto several times.

6. I (decide) to host a party.

   I have decided to host a party.

7. We (work) on archiving the documents for a five months now.

   We have worked on archiving the documents for five months now.

8. My sister (plays) softball for four years.

   My sister has played softball for four years.

Page 19

Answer Key

Page 20

Name _____ Date _____

Perfect Tenses

The present perfect tense tells about an action that starts in the past and has not yet ended. It can also tell about changes over time and life experiences. The present perfect tense uses the helping verb **has** or **have** with the past participle of a main verb.
   Present perfect: Davin **has played** the drums and piano since October.

The past perfect tense tells about an action that starts and ends in the past. The past perfect tense uses the helping verb **had** with the past participle of a main verb.
   Past perfect: Before that, he **had played** the violin and guitar.

The future perfect tense tells about an action that starts in the past and ends in the future. The future perfect tense uses the helping verbs **will have** with the past participle of a main verb.
   Future perfect: By next year, he **will have played** four instruments.

Rewrite each sentence. Use the perfect tense in the parentheses ( ) for the underlined verb.

1. My mom cook lasagna since I was little. (present perfect)
   My mom has cooked lasagna since I was little.

2. She learn to cook before I was born. (past perfect)
   She had learned to cook before I was born.

3. Mom boil about 100 pots of water by the end of this year! (future perfect)
   Mom will have boiled about 100 pots of water by the end of this year!

4. My mom dream of opening a restaurant for a long time. (present perfect)
   My mom has dreamed of opening a restaurant for a long time.

5. I hope for a clothing store instead of a restaurant. (past perfect)
   I had hoped for a clothing store instead of a restaurant.

6. I start drawing at the age of three. (past perfect)
   I had started drawing at the age of three.

7. My parents watch all of my games this year. (future perfect)
   My parents will have watched all of my games this year.

20   Conquer Grammar • Grade 5 • © Newmark Learning, LLC

Page 21

Name _____ Date _____

Subject-Verb Agreement

The subject of a sentence is a noun that tells who or what the sentence is about. The verb tells what the subject does. The subject and the verb in a sentence must agree. A singular subject takes a singular verb. A plural subject, including a compound subject, takes a plural verb.

   Singular Subject: He **is** a good painter.
   Plural Subject: A bird and a squirrel **live** in that big tree.

Complete each sentence. Choose the verb in the parentheses ( ) that agrees with the subject of the sentence and write it on the line.

1. Some of my neighbors _____*have*_____ a community garden.
   (have, has)

2. Ms. Consuelos _____*organizes*_____ the work in the garden.
   (organize, organizes)

3. However, many gardeners _____*share*_____ in its care.
   (share, shares)

4. In the spring, several folks _____*buy*_____ different kinds of seeds.
   (buy, buys)

5. This year, they _____*have voted*_____ to plant both vegetables and flowers.
   (has voted, have voted)

6. I _____*am planting*_____ cucumber seeds.
   (am planting, are planting)

7. Robert and Mary _____*are growing*_____ watermelons!
   (is growing, are growing)

8. The garden _____*has been*_____ a great way to bring our community together.
   (have been, has been)

21   Conquer Grammar • Grade 5 • © Newmark Learning, LLC

Page 22

Name _____ Date _____

Subject-Verb Agreement

The subject of a sentence is a noun that tells who or what the sentence is about. The verb tells what the subject does. The subject and the verb in a sentence must agree. A singular subject takes a singular verb. A plural subject, including a compound subject, takes a plural verb.

   Singular Subject: The boy **swims** in the pool.
   Plural Subject: Toy boats **float** nearby.

For each sentence, write Yes if the subject and verb agree. Write No if the subject and verb do not agree and then rewrite the sentence correctly.

1. __*No*__ My classmates and I does a lot of homework.
   My classmates and I do a lot of homework.

2. __*Yes*__ Denessa jogs two miles every Tuesday and Thursday after school.

3. __*No*__ I likes to play tennis at our town's tennis courts.
   I like to play tennis at our town's tennis courts.

4. __*No*__ Most kids in my class has joined one of the clubs at school.
   Most kids in my class have joined one of the clubs at school.

5. __*Yes*__ I see that many parents enjoy it, too.

6. __*No*__ My mom and my aunt practices yoga together on Saturday mornings.
   My mom and my aunt practice yoga together on Saturday mornings.

7. __*No*__ Yoga make them feel calm and focused.
   Yoga makes them feel calm and focused.

8. __*Yes*__ They also practice meditation at home.

22   Conquer Grammar • Grade 5 • © Newmark Learning, LLC

Page 23

Name _____ Date _____

Subject-Verb Agreement

The subject of a sentence is a noun that tells who or what the sentence is about. The verb tells what the subject does. The subject and the verb in a sentence must agree. A singular subject takes a singular verb. A plural subject, including a compound subject, takes a plural verb.
   Singular Subject: He **is** a good painter.
   Plural Subject: The trees in the park **are** beautiful.

Rewrite each sentence with correct subject-verb agreement.

1. A lion are coming out from behind the tree.
   A lion is coming out from behind the tree.

2. We needs to get out of here right now!
   We need to get out of here right now!

3. That aren't a lion after all.
   That isn't a lion after all.

4. That shadow look like an animal.
   That shadow looks like an animal.

5. We doesn't need to escape.
   We don't need to escape.

6. We is still safe.
   We are still safe.

7. We can eats our food now and enjoy it.
   We can eat our food now and enjoy it.

23   Conquer Grammar • Grade 5 • © Newmark Learning, LLC

Answer Key

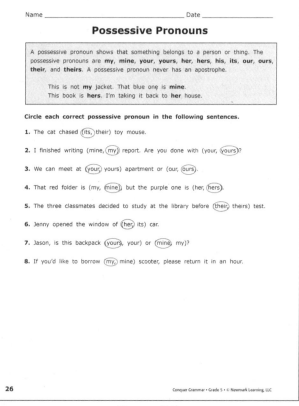

Page 24

Name _____ Date _____

Subject Pronouns

A pronoun is a word that takes the place of a noun. **I, you, she, he, it, we,** and **they** are subject pronouns. Use a subject pronoun when a pronoun is the subject of a sentence.

Incorrect: Him is my teacher.
Correct: He is my teacher.

Incorrect: My sister and **me** go skating on weekends.
Correct: My sister and **I** go skating on weekends.

Circle the correct subject pronoun in the parentheses ( ) to complete each sentence.

1. (They, Them) went to the movies and sat in the first row.

2. Chris and (I, me) will go to the game with you next week.

3. (Him, He) and (me, I) made it to the dance finals.

4. (Her, She) and Justine are sailing in the bay.

Underline each incorrect pronoun. Then rewrite the sentence with the correct subject pronoun.

5. Us and our cousins go fishing at the lake.
   We and our cousins go fishing at the lake.

6. Gino and me both sing in a choir.
   Gino and I both sing in a choir.

7. Sara and him made a pizza.
   Sara and he made a pizza.

8. My friend and me tutor younger students.
   My friend and I tutor younger students.

24   Conquer Grammar • Grade 5 • © Newmark Learning, LLC

Page 25

Name _____ Date _____

Object Pronouns

A pronoun is a word that takes the place of a noun. **Me, you, him, her, it, us,** and **them** are object pronouns. Use an object pronoun when a pronoun is the object of a verb or a preposition.

Incorrect: The music teacher gave an award to Laila and **I**.
Correct: The music teacher gave an award to Laila and **me**.

Incorrect: This is a key competition for us and **they**.
Correct: This is a key competition for us and **them**.

Circle the correct object pronoun in the parentheses ( ) to complete each sentence.

1. James rides the roller coaster with my sister and (I, me).

2. The rain delayed the game between (we, us) and (them, they).

3. Ariel made cookies for you and (we, us).

4. Postcards arrived for both (he, him) and his brother.

Underline each incorrect pronoun. Then rewrite the sentence with the correct object pronoun.

5. Melanie went to the concert with Taryn and I.
   Melanie went to the concert with Taryn and me.

6. The teacher gave he and her a surprise quiz.
   The teacher gave him and her a surprise quiz.

7. Andrew brought Natalie and I some popcorn.
   Andrew brought Natalie and me some popcorn.

8. Please remember to call they tomorrow.
   Please remember to call them tomorrow.

Conquer Grammar • Grade 5 • © Newmark Learning, LLC   25

Page 26

Name _____ Date _____

Possessive Pronouns

A possessive pronoun shows that something belongs to a person or thing. The possessive pronouns are **my, mine, your, yours, her, hers, his, its, our, ours, their,** and **theirs**. A possessive pronoun never has an apostrophe.

This is not **my** jacket. That blue one is **mine**.
This book is **hers**. I'm taking it back to **her** house.

Circle each correct possessive pronoun in the following sentences.

1. The cat chased (its, their) toy mouse.

2. I finished writing (mine, my) report. Are you done with (your, yours)?

3. We can meet at (your, yours) apartment or (our, ours).

4. That red folder is (my, mine) but the purple one is (her, hers).

5. The three classmates decided to study at the library before (their, theirs) test.

6. Jenny opened the window of (her, its) car.

7. Jason, is this backpack (yours, your) or (mine, my)?

8. If you'd like to borrow (my, mine) scooter, please return it in an hour.

26   Conquer Grammar • Grade 5 • © Newmark Learning, LLC

Page 27

Name _____ Date _____

Interrogative Pronouns and Relative Pronouns

Use an interrogative pronoun, such as **who, whom, what, which,** and **whose** to introduce a question.
Use a relative pronoun such as **who, whom, whose, that,** and **which** to introduce a relative clause that tells more information about a word in the sentence.

Interrogative pronouns: What are your plans tomorrow? **Which** exhibit would you like to see? **Who** else would like to come? **Whose** mom is taking us to the museum?

Relative pronouns: The 3-D movie, **which** my sister has seen, is very good. My friend **who** lives around the corner may be late. We can wear the friendship bracelets **that** you made.

Circle the correct interrogative pronoun in ( ) and the correct relative pronoun in ( ) to complete each sentence.

1. (Who, What) wants to see the play (whom, that) Alejandro recommended?

2. (Which, Who) dog is the one (which, that) buried the bone?

3. (Who, Whose) wants to surf at Mission Beach, (which, who) happens to be my favorite beach?

4. (Whose, Who) recreation center is the one (whose, that) has a swimming pool?

5. (What, Which) friend is the one (that, who) plays soccer with you?

6. (Who, What) would like the extra apple (whose, that) I brought?

Conquer Grammar • Grade 5 • © Newmark Learning, LLC   27

Answer Key

Name _____ Date _____

Pronoun-Antecedent Agreement

The noun that a pronoun replaces is called an antecedent. A pronoun and its antecedent must match in number and person.

Incorrect: Before **Tim** gets lost, **they** should check a map.
Correct: Before **Tim** gets lost, **he** should check a map.

Read each sentence and circle the pronoun that is correct in number.

1. You should proofread (you, (your) yours) book report before you turn it in.

2. Nina and I brought (their, she, (our)) sleeping bags for the slumber party.

3. The fifth grade classes had a meeting about (its, (their), they) bake sale.

4. After a nap, the cat found (theirs, their, (its)) toy and began to play.

5. This time, the parents agreed with (his, her, (their)) children.

6. At ((its) yours, his) last rehearsal, the school choir held auditions for the big solo.

7. Dina and Dana were late for practice because (we, she, (they)) forgot to set the alarm.

8. Justin read a biography about (himself, he, (his)) favorite musician.

28
Conquer Grammar • Grade 5 • © Newmark Learning, LLC

Page 28

Name _____ Date _____

Pronoun-Antecedent Agreement

The noun that a pronoun replaces is called an antecedent. A pronoun and its antecedent must match in number and person.

	Pronoun	Antecedent	Agreement
I hung the coat in **my** closet.	my	I	singular, first person
Kendra, here is **your** notebook.	your	Kendra	singular, second person
The **citizens** wanted to help, so **they** organized a community clean-up day.	they	Citizens	plural, third person

Write the pronoun that correctly completes the sentence.

1. The newest member of team, Lucy, gave _____her_____ best effort yet.

2. The judges could not agree on _____their_____ choice for first place.

3. You should think about the consequences of _____your_____ actions.

4. Alaska is the largest state by area, but _____it_____ does not have the largest population.

5. If people work together, _____they_____ should finish the job quickly.

6. It was raining when Mark realized that _____he_____ had forgotten an umbrella.

29
Conquer Grammar • Grade 5 • © Newmark Learning, LLC

Page 29

Name _____ Date _____

Adjectives

Adjectives are words that describe nouns. They tell about size, color, number, and kind. Follow this order when using more than one adjective to describe a noun: number (eight, many), opinion (kind, funny, tasty), size (huge, small), looks/feels (bumpy, soft), age (new, ancient), color (red, yellow), origin (American, Mexican), material (metal, cotton). Place a comma after each adjective, except a number and between the last adjective and the noun.

Incorrect: We have **two, energetic, young** puppies with **long, fuzzy,** ears.
Correct: We have **two energetic, young** puppies with **long, fuzzy** ears.

Complete each sentence. Write the adjectives in the parentheses ( ) in the correct order.

1. The _____cute_____, _____fluffy_____, _____colorful_____ bunny wiggled its nose at me.
   (fluffy white cute)

2. Did you see the _____tall_____, _____colorful_____ flowers in the garden?
   (colorful tall)

3. I ordered a _____tasty_____, _____big_____, _____Italian_____ pizza.
   (big Italian tasty)

4. Tony got a _____wonderful_____, _____shiny_____, _____red_____ bike for his birthday.
   (red wonderful shiny)

5. A _____small_____, _____striped_____ bird flew in front of me.
   (striped small)

6. Did anyone sit on the _____fancy_____, _____new_____, _____white_____ sofa?
   (white fancy new)

30
Conquer Grammar • Grade 5 • © Newmark Learning, LLC

Page 30

Name _____ Date _____

Adjectives

Adjectives are words that describe nouns. They tell about size, color, number, and kind. Follow this order when using more than one adjective to describe a noun: number (four, few), opinion (beautiful, special), size (tiny, wide), looks/feels (warm, bumpy), age (new, old), shape (oblong, pointed) color (gray, blue), origin (Alaskan, Egyptian), material (paper, glass). Place a comma after each adjective, except a number and between the last adjective and the noun.

Incorrect: I have **two, furry, amazing, large,** dogs.
Correct: I have **two amazing, large, furry** dogs.

Circle the adjectives that are in the correct order. Rewrite the adjectives on the line with commas.

1. Mike always takes his _____practical, black, canvas_____ bag to the gym.
   a. practical black canvas b. black practical canvas

2. I'm going to cook _____two delicious, thick_____ steaks.
   a. delicious thick two b. two delicious thick

3. We saw a film about _____five smart, teenage_____ children who live in Chicago.
   a. five teenage smart b. five smart teenage

4. We bought _____three fluffy, multicolored_____ towels for our beach vacation.
   a. three fluffy multicolored b. multicolored fluffy three

5. Junior took pictures of _____several enormous, gray_____ whales.
   a. several enormous gray b. several gray enormous

6. The mural is made of _____many small, smooth, glass_____ tiles.
   a. many smooth glass small b. many small smooth glass

31
Conquer Grammar • Grade 5 • © Newmark Learning, LLC

Page 31

Answer Key

Page 32

Adjectives

Adjectives are words that describe nouns. They tell about size, color, number, and kind. Follow this order when using more than one adjective to describe a noun: number (nine, many, several), opinion (honest, friendly), size (titanic, microscopic), looks/feels (sticky, prickly), age (recent, modern), shape (round, triangular), color (pastel, translucent), origin (Chinese, Kenyan), material (straw, wooden). Place a comma after each adjective, except a number and between the last adjective and the noun.

Incorrect: My dog Jackson wore **two, old, red, cotton,** bandannas.
Correct: My dog Jackson wore **two old, red, cotton** bandannas.

Add the given adjectives to each sentence. Write them in the correct order with commas.

1. I need to return the _three thick, musty, old_ books to the library.
   thick   musty   three   old

2. Beau and Jasper are Uncle Larry's _two curious, spotted_ hounds.
   spotted   curious   two

3. I placed _many tiny, round_ seeds in my garden.
   round   many   tiny

4. The reporter interviewed _four concerned, longtime_ residents of the neighborhood.
   four   longtime   concerned

5. The sun looked like a _sizzling, round, orange_ ball against the evening sky.
   orange   round   sizzling

6. The _two awkward, newborn_ calves stood up in the pasture.
   newborn   awkward   two

Page 33

Adverbs

Adverbs give more information about where or when an action occurs or how it happens. An adverb can appear before or after the verb it modifies or in between different verb parts.

Where: Our neighbors came **around** for a party.
When: Soon, summer will be over.
How: The sun was still shining **brightly** in the sky.

Circle the adverb in each sentence. Then write if it shows where, when, or how the action happens.

1. The athletes ran (quickly) around the oval track. _how_

2. We sat (uncomfortably) on the hard, metal bleachers. _how_

3. Thanks to the wind, leaves were blowing (everywhere). _where_

4. The team competes at track meets (weekly). _when_

5. The fans cheer (loudly) for their favorite competitors. _how_

6. (Later,) we will share a pizza with our friends. _when_

7. (Yesterday,) I got a haircut. _when_

8. The team met (eagerly) at the finish line. _how_

Page 34

Relative Adverbs

A relative adverb introduces a relative clause and refers to a time, a place, or a reason. The relative clause gives more information about a word or phrase in the sentence. The words **when**, **where**, and **why** may be used as relative adverbs.

Time: June is usually the month **when** the rose bushes bloom.
Place: Minnesota is **where** my cousins live.
Reason: I know the reason **why** I am so tired today.

Underline the relative clause in each sentence. Circle the relative adverb.

1. Our father explained the reason (why) our family was moving.

2. I went to camp, (where) I learned to ride a horse.

3. Last year was (when) my sister started kindergarten.

4. Tuesday is (when) I have my trumpet lesson.

5. Florida is (where) my grandparents live.

6. I'll always remember (when) I lost my first tooth.

Page 35

Prepositions

A preposition shows the relationship between a noun or pronoun and another word in a sentence. The relationship may show **what**, **when**, **where**, or **how**. Some common prepositions are **about, above, across, after, against, around, at, before, behind, below, beside, between, by, during, for, from, in, near, of, on, out, over, through, to, under, until, up, with**.

The cat napped **after** his meal.
The book is **on** the table **beside** the lamp.

Underline the prepositions in each sentence.

1. We went hiking with our parents.

2. James walked under the trees, which were green and leafy.

3. The pollen flew around us, and it drifted into my nose.

4. At the store, Franklin found the muffin mix above the regular flour.

5. In the next aisle, beside the apples, we found the lemons.

Complete each sentence with a preposition that matches the relationship in the parentheses ( ).

6. They'll go home on the bus _after_ the movie ends. (when)

7. The dog was hiding _under_ the chair. (where)

8. Our class is making bridges _with_ glue and craft sticks. (how)

Answer Key

Page 36

Name _____ Date _____

Prepositions

A preposition shows the relationship between a noun or pronoun and another word in a sentence. The relationship may show **what, when, where,** or **how.** Some common prepositions are **about, above, across, after, against, around, at, before, behind, below, beside, between, by, during, for, from, in, near, of, on, out, over, through, to, under, until, up, with.**

After <u>lunch</u>, I'll return **with** <u>treats</u>.

Underline the prepositions in each sentence.

1. <u>After</u> dinner, we took our three dogs <u>for</u> a walk.

2. They ran <u>down</u> the block and <u>around</u> our corner.

3. They stopped <u>beside</u> a bush <u>near</u> a fence.

4. We ran <u>toward</u> them, and they gazed <u>at</u> us hopefully.

5. We reached for some treats <u>in</u> our bag, and the dogs jumped <u>with</u> joy.

Complete each sentence with a preposition that matches the relationship in the parentheses ( ).

6. Bella carried the trunk _____up_____ the stairs to the attic. (where)

7. Do you want to go to the library _____before_____ lunch or after lunch? (when)

8. Junior drove carefully into a parking space _____between_____ two parked cars. (where)

9. I strolled _____around_____ the bookstore. (where)

10. I read _____with_____ great interest. (how)

Conquer Grammar • Grade 5 • © Newmark Learning, LLC

Page 37

Name _____ Date _____

Prepositions

A preposition shows the relationship between the noun or pronoun and another word in the sentence. The relationship may show **what, when, where, how,** or **how long.** Some common prepositions are **above, about, across, after, around, at, before, between, by, down, for, in, into, on, of, to, toward, under, up, at,** and **with.**

I saw a pair **of** <u>goats</u> running **around** a <u>fenced-in field</u>.
I watched them **for** <u>a few minutes</u>.

Circle the preposition in each sentence and underline the noun phrase that relates to the preposition.

1. Marley took us (into) <u>the living room</u>.

2. She told us (about) <u>her new puppy</u>.

3. The kitten, named Baxter, was curled up (under) <u>a desk</u>.

4. Tail wagging, Baxter barked (at) <u>us</u>.

Complete each sentence with a preposition that matches the relationship in the parentheses ( ).

5. We will have a celebration _____in_____ the park. (where)

6. All the classes will go to Sunset View Park _____by_____ bus. (how)

7. We'll get there _____between_____ 10 a.m. and 10:15 a.m. (when)

8. We'll barbecue and play games _____for_____ a few hours. (how long)

Conquer Grammar • Grade 5 • © Newmark Learning, LLC

Page 38

Name _____ Date _____

Prepositions

A preposition shows the relationship between a noun or pronoun and another word in a sentence. The relationship may show **what, when, where,** or **how.** Some common prepositions are **about, above, across, after, against, around, at, before, behind, below, beside, between, by, during, for, from, in, near, of, on, out, over, through, to, under, until, up, with.**

Christina walked **through** <u>the narrow opening</u>.

Circle the preposition in each sentence and underline the noun that relates to the preposition.

1. Marco appeared (in) <u>the talent show</u>.

2. He had news (about) <u>a holiday sale</u> at the mall.

3. School buses were parked (behind) <u>the cafeteria</u>.

4. We have math class (after) <u>lunch</u>.

Write the correct preposition to complete each sentence. Then underline the noun phrase that relates to the preposition.

5. We read a story _____about_____ <u>the Great Blizzard</u>.

6. The storm began _____on_____ <u>March 11, 1888</u>.

7. It snowed _____for_____ <u>three days</u>.

8. The river was frozen _____with_____ <u>thick ice</u>.

9. Therefore, people were able to walk _____on_____ <u>the river</u>.

10. Some snowdrifts lasted _____until_____ <u>July 4</u>!

Conquer Grammar • Grade 5 • © Newmark Learning, LLC

Page 39

Name _____ Date _____

Prepositions

A preposition shows the relationship between a noun or pronoun and another word in a sentence. The relationship may show **what, when, where,** or **how.** Some common prepositions are **about, above, across, after, against, around, at, before, behind, below, beside, between, by, during, for, from, in, near, of, on, out, over, through, to, under, until, up, with.**

My dog curled up **beside** <u>me</u> **on** <u>the couch</u>.

Write a preposition or prepositions to complete each sentence. Choose one of the following: *from, with, at, into, through, for.*

1. I went _____with_____ my friend Lee to the mall.

2. We were coming _____from_____ his house.

3. As we walked _____through_____ the door of one store, we heard a bell ring.

4. The clerk working _____at_____ the counter greeted us.

5. We went to the sweater section _____at_____ the back of the store.

6. We selected what we needed _____from_____ the racks and brought it _____into_____ the fitting room.

7. Then, I looked _____through_____ my backpack, searching _____for_____ my money.

8. Oh, no! I must have left my wallet _____at_____ Lee's house.

9. I should have remembered to bring it _____with_____ me.

10. Lee got his wallet _____from_____ his pocket.

Conquer Grammar • Grade 5 • © Newmark Learning, LLC

Conquer Grammar • Grade 5 • © Newmark Learning, LLC

Answer Key

Page 40

Name _____ Date _____

Correlative Conjunctions

Correlative conjunctions always come in pairs and appear in different parts of a sentence. They work together to connect the parts of the sentence. Use the correlative conjunctions **both...and** to add one idea to another. **Either...or** gives an alternative. **Neither...nor** gives no alternative. **Not only...but also** contrasts two ideas.

We'll go **either** to a cafeteria **or** to a restaurant.
Both my cousin **and** my sister came with me to the movies.
Neither my sister **nor** my cousin liked the movie.
They said they had wasted **not** one **but** two weeks of allowance.
They were **not only** frustrated **but also** irritated.

Underline the correlative conjunctions in each sentence.

1. You can <u>either</u> play volleyball <u>or</u> swim laps in the pool.

2. The event will be <u>both</u> more meaningful <u>and</u> more enjoyable if you join us.

3. We will go <u>neither</u> to the skating rink <u>nor</u> to the bowling alley.

4. We will go <u>either</u> to the zoo <u>or</u> to the amusement park.

5. Not only will you learn something, <u>but also</u> you will ace the test.

Rewrite each pair of sentences as one sentence. Use the correlative conjunctions in the parentheses ( ).

6. Tessa likes historical fiction. Tessa also likes tall tales. (both...and)

   Tessa likes both historical fiction and tall tales.

7. Gabby can bring pasta salad. Gabby can bring macaroni and cheese. (either...or)

   Gabby can bring either pasta salad or macaroni and cheese.

40   Conquer Grammar • Grade 5 • © Newmark Learning, LLC

Page 41

Name _____ Date _____

Correlative Conjunctions

Correlative conjunctions always come in pairs and appear in different parts of a sentence. They work together to connect the parts of the sentence. Use the correlative conjunctions **both...and** to add one idea to another. **Either...or** gives an alternative. **Neither...nor** gives no alternative. **Not only...but also** contrasts two ideas.

Both Morgan **and** Lucy want a pet.
Either a cat **or** a dog would make a good pet.
Neither Morgan **nor** Lucy has time to walk a dog.
They adopted a cat that's **not only** beautiful **but also** friendly.

In each sentence, determine the missing half of the correlative conjunction. Write the missing part on the line to complete the sentence.

1. We'll either all take a bus ___ _or_ ___ we'll all bike to the park.

2. ___ _Both_ ___ Suzette and Louis are going to be there later.

3. The party invitation said not to bring gifts ___ _but_ ___ instead to make homemade cards or treats.

4. Neither the popcorn you're bringing ___ _nor_ ___ the lemonade will spoil if left out.

5. Both the food ___ _and_ ___ the cards are on the table.

6. We will see not only our friends ___ _but also_ ___ our family!

7. ___ _Neither_ ___ Rowena nor Anthony will be able to come.

8. ___ _Neither_ ___ Marianne nor Mike are driving hours to be there.

Conquer Grammar • Grade 5 • © Newmark Learning, LLC   41

Page 42

Name _____ Date _____

Correlative Conjunctions

Correlative conjunctions always come in pairs and appear in different parts of a sentence. They work together to connect the parts of the sentence. Use the correlative conjunctions **both...and** to add one idea to another. **Either...or** gives an alternative. **Neither...nor** gives no alternative. **Not only...but also** contrasts two ideas.

I can wear **either** shorts **or** jeans to play many sports.
I can wear **neither** shorts **nor** jeans to my uncle's wedding.

Write two sentences to answer each question. Use the correlative conjunctions *either...or* in the first sentence and *neither...nor* in the second sentence.

1. Do you want a hamburger? Do you want a hot dog?
   I want either a hamburger or a hot dog.
   I want neither a hot dog nor a hamburger.

2. Should we go to the beach or to the mountains?
   We should go either to the beach or to the mountains.
   We should go neither to the beach nor to the mountains.

Rewrite each pair of sentences with the correlative conjunctions *either...or* or *neither...nor*.

3. A prairie dog is not a dog. It is not a gopher.
   A prairie dog is neither a dog nor a gopher.

4. They do not bark. They do not squeak.
   They neither bark nor squeak.

5. Prairie dogs yip. They whistle too.
   Prairie dogs either yip or whistle.

6. Prairie dogs move into existing burrows. Prairie dogs dig new ones.
   Prairie dogs either move into existing burrows or dig new ones.

42   Conquer Grammar • Grade 5 • © Newmark Learning, LLC

Page 43

Name _____ Date _____

Correlative Conjunctions

Correlative conjunctions always come in pairs and appear in different parts of a sentence. They work together to connect the parts of the sentence. Use the correlative conjunctions **both...and** to add one idea to another. **Either...or** gives an alternative. **Neither...nor** gives no alternative. **Not only...but also** contrasts two ideas.

I like **both** jam **and** jelly.
Either butter **or** tomato sauce would taste good on the pasta.

Rewrite each pair of sentences as one sentence. Use the correlative conjunctions in the parentheses ( ).

1. At the bakery, the smell of bread was savory. The smell was strong. (both...and)
   At the bakery, the smell of bread was both savory and strong.

2. Sherry offered us cider. Sherry offered us lemonade. (either...or)
   Sherry offered us either cider or lemonade.

3. They would like the salad. I would like the soup. (not only...but also)
   They would like not only the salad but also the soup.

4. When they left, they were not thirsty. They were not hungry. (neither...nor)
   When they left, they were neither thirsty nor hungry.

5. This field trip was informative. It was fun. (not only...but also)
   This field trip was not only informative but also fun.

Conquer Grammar • Grade 5 • © Newmark Learning, LLC   43

Answer Key

Page 44

Name _____ Date _____

Correlative Conjunctions

Correlative conjunctions always come in pairs and appear in different parts of a sentence. They work together to connect the parts of the sentence. Use the correlative conjunctions **both...and** to add one idea to another. **Either...or** gives an alternative. **Neither...nor** gives no alternative. **Not only...but also** contrasts two ideas.

   Both Rosie **and** Manny came to the movies with us.
   Afterward, we had **not only** pizza **but also** dessert.

Join each pair of independent clauses with the correlative conjunctions in the parentheses ( ). Write the sentence on the line.

1. Sunday was sunny. It was breezy. (both...and)

   Sunday was both sunny and breezy.

2. We could go to the beach. We could fly a kite. (either...or)

   We could either go to the beach or fly a kite.

3. Luca did not want to fly a kite. Max did not want to fly a kite. (neither...nor)

   Neither Luca nor Max wanted to fly a kite.

4. At the beach, I swam. I flew the kite along the shore. (both...and)

   At the beach, I both swam and flew the kite along the shore.

5. I had a delightful day. I got a lot of exercise. (not only...but also)

   I not only had a delightful day but also got a lot of exercise.

6. I was exhausted. I was hungry. (not only...but also)

   I was not only exhausted but also hungry.

Page 45

Name _____ Date _____

Commas for Introductory Phrases

When a sentence begins with an introductory phrase, use a comma to set off the phrase from the rest of the sentence.
   At dawn, we could hear the birds begin to sing.

Underline the introductory phrase in each sentence.

1. Before I go, I should make sure I have everything with me.

2. After school, let's eat a snack.

3. Since I am hungry now, I already have something prepared.

4. Because of the time, we should probably catch the bus soon.

5. As he was the first person in line for the movie, Clarence had his choice of seats.

6. In the center section, he'll have the best view of the screen.

Rewrite each sentence. Add a comma to set off the introductory phrase.

7. Even with Patrice's goal the team lost the playoff game.

   Even with Patrice's goal, the team lost the playoff game.

8. Next season we'll do better.

   Next season, we'll do better.

Page 46

Name _____ Date _____

Commas for Introductory Phrases

When a sentence begins with an introductory phrase, use a comma to set off the phrase from the rest of the sentence.
   Most years, the cherry trees are in full bloom in April.

Rewrite each sentence. Add a comma to set off the introductory phrase.

1. In my opinion the ballet performance was lovely.

   In my opinion, the ballet performance was lovely.

2. In fact the whole audience seemed to agree.

   In fact, the whole audience seemed to agree.

3. In the beginning I wasn't sure that the ballerinas would be good.

   In the beginning, I wasn't sure that the ballerinas would be good.

4. However I was so wrong!

   However, I was so wrong!

5. During intermission two young ballerinas peeked out from behind the curtain.

   During intermission, two young ballerinas peeked out from behind the curtain.

6. At the end some fans tossed single roses onto the stage.

   At the end, some fans tossed single roses onto the stage.

7. Honestly it was the finest performance I've ever seen!

   Honestly, it was the finest performance I've ever seen!

8. Believe it or not I danced and twirled all the way home.

   Believe it or not, I danced and twirled all the way home.

Page 47

Name _____ Date _____

Commas for Introductory Phrases

When a sentence begins with an introductory phrase, use a comma to set off the phrase from the rest of the sentence.
   In the first book of the trilogy, the explorers see something shocking.

Rewrite each sentence. Add a comma to set off the introductory phrase.

1. As a lover of science I found this research fascinating.

   As a lover of science, I found this research fascinating.

2. Once I am inside the laboratory I put on my safety goggles.

   Once I am inside the laboratory, I put on my safety goggles.

3. Every afternoon light shines through the western windows.

   Every afternoon, light comes through the western windows.

4. Because of the strong sunlight I sometimes lower the window shades.

   Because of the strong sunlight, I sometimes lower the window shades.

5. Despite some frightening scenes horror novels appeal to me.

   Despite some frightening scenes, horror novels appeal to me.

6. With so much to do this week I cannot visit the library.

   With so much to do this week, I cannot visit the library.

Answer Key

Page 48

Commas

> Within a sentence, commas are used to set off introductory words or phrases, separate words in a series or list, and divide two independent clauses joined by a coordinating conjunction such as **and** or **but**.
>
> In fact, I saw Ravi, Joaquin, and Amy at recess, but my other friends were not there.

For each sentence, write the element that the comma or commas sets off: *introductory phrase, words in a series,* or *two independent clauses.*

1. My family went to the zoo, and I was eager to see the reptiles.
    two independent clauses

2. Prior to this visit, we had never been to the zoo.
    introductory phrase

3. First we saw jaguars, cheetahs, and apes.
    words in a series

4. My favorite animal was the giraffe, but my sister's favorite was the baby hippo.
    two independent clauses

5. We were excited to see the exhibits, visit the gift shop, and buy some trinkets.
    words in a series

6. After such a fun day, we asked if we could visit the aquarium next year.
    introductory phrase

Rewrite each sentence. Add commas where needed.

7. I saw roses daffodils and daisies but I couldn't decide which ones to buy.
    I saw roses, daffodils, and daisies, but I couldn't decide which ones to buy.

8. After staying up late I was really tired for the entire day.
    After staying up late, I was really tired for the entire day.

Page 49

Commas

> Within a sentence, commas are used to set off introductory words or phrases and to separate three or more items listed in a series. A comma is often used to separate two independent clauses joined by **and**, **but**, or **so** in a compound sentence.
>
> All week, we planted bulbs, so we will have daffodils, tulips, and irises next spring.

Add the necessary commas to each sentence.

1. In the morning, Lily woke at sunrise.

2. She was going to the beach, but first she needed to prepare.

3. She packed sunscreen, sandwiches, and a striped beach umbrella.

4. At first, she couldn't find anywhere to spread out her beach towels.

5. She found a spot right by the lifeguard tower, and it was perfect.

6. She watched the seagulls swoop, soar, and dive into the ocean to catch a fish.

Rewrite each sentence. Add commas where needed.

7. In the late afternoon a nearby family packed up their blanket towels and umbrella but there was no food left to take home.

    In the late afternoon, a nearby family packed up their blanket, towels, and umbrella, but there was no food left to take home.

8. After a short wait the bus came and Sasha Nate and I got on with our stuff.

    After a short wait, the bus came, and Sasha, Nate, and I got on with our stuff.

Page 50

Commas

> Within a sentence, commas are used to set off introductory words or phrases, separate words in a series or list, and divide two independent clauses joined by a coordinating conjunction such as **and** or **but**.
>
> At the store, he bought fruit, eggs, and cheese, but he forgot to get milk.

Add commas to each sentence. Then determine whether the comma or commas set off an introductory phrase, words in a series, two independent clauses, or a combination of the three. Write *I* for introductory phrase, *S* for series, *C* for compound sentence.

1. I studied algebra, geometry, and measurement. __S__

2. In the beginning, Jason liked Ms. Wilson's chemistry class best. __I__

3. Later on, he found that he also enjoyed history, but he still liked chemistry more. __I__ __C__

4. The bell rang at 2:15 p.m., and we went outside to play volleyball. __C__

5. At first, Chris and I scored the most points, but then Micah and Joelle outscored us. __I__ __C__

6. It was fun, so Joelle, Micah, and Chris decided to play every week. __C__ __S__

7. I enjoy the time I spend with my mom, dad, and brothers. __S__

8. When I got home, I took a long bath. __I__

Page 51

Commas

> Within a sentence, commas are used to set off introductory words or phrases, separate words in a series or list, and divide two independent clauses joined by a coordinating conjunction such as **and** or **but**.
>
> Wow, that was such an exciting adventure movie!
> I have to buy lemons, limes, sugar, and a pitcher.
> It started to rain, but Sergio had his umbrella.

Rewrite each sentence. Add commas where needed.

1. Earlier the doorbell rang.
    Earlier, the doorbell rang.

2. Nicole Marcus and Tommy had arrived.
    Nicole, Marcus, and Tommy had arrived.

3. Tommy wanted to do homework but Nicole wanted to watch funny videos.
    Tommy wanted to do homework, but Nicole wanted to watch funny videos.

4. We took out our textbooks our notes and our pencils.
    We took out our textbooks, our notes, and our pencils.

5. The next thing we knew our work was done and we could watch some videos.
    The next thing we knew, our work was done, and we could watch some videos.

6. Marcus recommended his favorites and we spent the rest of the afternoon laughing.
    Marcus recommended his favorites, and we spent the rest of the afternoon laughing.

Answer Key

Page 52

Commas

Use commas to separate three or more items in a series, and before the conjunction **and** or **or** in a series.
I can't decide between **a veggie burger, sushi, or soup** for lunch.
Please buy **a bag of potatoes, a box of tea, and a gallon of milk**.
My uncle ran in the **2009, 2010, 2011, and 2013** Boston marathons.

Rewrite each sentence. Add commas where needed.

1. We will serve fried chicken macaroni salad and juice at the birthday party.
   We will serve fried chicken, macaroni salad, and juice at the birthday party.

2. We decorated the party room on Thursday Friday and Saturday.
   We decorated the party room on Thursday, Friday, and Saturday.

3. We have red blue and yellow streamers.
   We have red, blue, and yellow streamers.

4. Dozens of balloons were purchased inflated and tied up by noon on Saturday.
   Dozens of balloons were purchased, inflated, and tied up by noon on Saturday.

5. We could smell the aroma of the food cooking from the living room the dining room and the hallway.
   We could smell the aroma of the food cooking from the living room,
   the dining room, and the hallway.

6. Decorations friends and delicious food make parties fun!
   Decorations, friends, and delicious food make parties fun!

7. The guests gathered in the living room the kitchen and the yard.
   The guests gathered in the living room, the kitchen, and the yard.

Page 53

Commas in Dialogue

If the speaker is identified before the dialogue, place a comma after the speaker's tag. If the speaker is introduced after the dialogue, place a comma inside the final quotation mark. Drop the comma, however, if the quote ends in a question mark or an exclamation point.
Soraya asked, "Do you see the bus?"
"I don't see it coming," answered Alex.

Rewrite each sentence. Add commas where needed.

1. Julio asked "Dad, can Byron and I go to a movie?"
   Julio asked, "Dad, can Byron and I go to a movie?"

2. Dad asked "Have you put away the dishes?"
   Dad asked, "Have you put away the dishes?"

3. "I put everything away" answered Julio.
   "I put everything away," answered Julio.

4. Dad said "That's great! Have fun."
   Dad said, "That's great! Have fun."

5. "Thanks! I'll let you know how I liked it" said Julio.
   "Thanks! I'll let you know how I liked it," said Julio.

6. Byron said "I'll buy the popcorn!"
   Byron said, "I'll buy the popcorn!"

7. "Don't have too much junk food" Mom said.
   "Don't have too much junk food," Mom said.

8. "We won't, we promise" Julio said.
   "We won't, we promise," Julio said.

Page 54

Commas in Dialogue

Purpose of Comma in Dialogue	Example
to indicate direct address	"Spence, do you want to walk?"
to set off introductory words like **yes** or **no**	"No, my science project is too fragile."
to set off a tag question	"We will walk home, won't we?"

Rewrite each sentence. Add commas where needed.

1. "Are you trying out for choir Jeannie?" asked Carmela.
   "Are you trying out for choir, Jeannie?" asked Carmela.

2. "Yes here is the song I want to sing" she said.
   "Yes, here is the song I want to sing," she said.

3. Carmela said "Oh that's the same song I planned to sing!"
   Carmela said, "Oh, that's the same song I planned to sing!"

4. Jeannie said "We can both sing it can't we?"
   Jeannie said, "We can both sing it, can't we?"

5. "I have an idea. Let's sing it as a duet" said Jeannie.
   "I have an idea. Let's sing it as a duet," said Jeannie.

6. Carmela replied "Yes that would be memorable right?"
   Carmela replied, "Yes, that would be memorable, right?"

7. "Exactly that is a good compromise," Jeannie said.
   "Exactly, that is a good compromise," Jeannie said.

8. "I am excited to sing with you Jeannie!" Carmela replied.
   "I am excited to sing with you, Jeannie!" Carmela replied.

Page 55

Commas in Dialogue

Purpose of Comma in Dialogue	Example
to set off the speaker's tag: if the speaker is identified before the dialogue, place a comma after the speaker's tag.	**Simone said**, "I don't see the train."
to set off the speaker's tag: if the speaker is identified after the dialogue, place a comma inside the final quotation mark.	"I don't see it either," **replied Olivia.**
to indicate direct address	Simone said, "**Olivia,** I think you won!"
to set off introductory words like **yes** or **no**	Olivia said, "**No,** I didn't!"
to set off a tag question	"We will walk home, **won't we?**"

Rewrite each sentence. Add commas where needed.

1. Elias asked his sister "Which park should we go to Ava?"
   Elias asked his sister, "Which park should we go to, Ava?"

2. Ava said "Let's go to the one with the pool okay?"
   Ava said, "Let's go to the one with the pool, okay?"

3. Elias said "No I think that one is too far."
   Elias said, "No, I think that one is too far."

4. "Well the one with the bike trail is closer isn't it?" Ava said.
   "Well, the one with the bike trail is closer, isn't it?" Ava said.

5. "Yep and it's a perfect day for riding bikes" said Elias.
   "Yep, and it's a perfect day for riding bikes," said Elias.

6. Ava said "Wow this is going to be a fun day!"
   Ava said, "Wow, this is going to be a fun day!"

7. Elias said "Yes I am so excited!"
   Elias said, "Yes, I am so excited!"

8. Ava asked her brother "Should we leave now Elias?"
   Ava asked her brother, "Should we leave now, Elias?"

Answer Key

Name _____ Date _____

Commas in Dialogue

Purpose of Comma in Dialogue	Example
to set off the speaker's tag: if the speaker is identified before the dialogue, place a comma after the speaker's tag.	**Gisele said,** "Cory, let's get lunch, okay?"
to set off the speaker's tag: if the speaker is identified after the dialogue, place a comma inside the final quotation mark.	"I liked the movie," **George said.**
to indicate direct address	Taylor asked, "**Mary,** how are you?"
to set off introductory words like **yes** or **no**	Beth said, "**Yes,** of course I will come with you."
to set off a tag question	"We will go to the store, **won't we?"**

Rewrite each sentence. Add commas where needed.

1. Jody asked "What time do we have to be at the event?"

   Jody asked, "What time do we have to be at the event?"

2. Scott said, "We should be there by noon Jody."

   Scott said, "We should be there by noon, Jody."

3. Jody asked "Should we leave in an hour?"

   Jody asked, "Should we leave in an hour?"

4. "Yes I'll go gather my things," Scott answered.

   "Yes, I'll go gather my things," Scott answered.

5. "Sharee will be at the event won't she?" Scott asked.

   "Sharee will be at the event, won't she?" Scott asked.

Conquer Grammar • Grade 5 • © Newmark Learning, LLC

Page 56

Name _____ Date _____

Punctuate Quotations

A quotation is the exact words spoken by a real person. Use quotation marks to set off the speaker's exact words. If the person being quoted is identified first, place a comma before the first quotation mark. If the person being quoted is identified after the quote, place a comma inside the final quotation mark. Place periods inside quotation marks. If the quote itself ends in a question mark or an exclamation point, place the punctuation inside the final quotation mark and drop the comma. Always capitalize the first word in the quotation marks. If the quote is interrupted, do not capitalize the first word in the continuation.

President Roosevelt said, "The only thing we have to fear is fear itself."

Each sentence below contains a quote. Rewrite each sentence with proper punctuation and capitalization.

1. My violin teacher used to say practice makes perfect.

   My violin teacher used to say, "Practice makes perfect."

2. Mark Twain once said the secret to getting ahead is getting started.

   Mark Twain once said, "The secret to getting ahead is getting started."

3. Mother always claims the early bird catches the worm.

   Mother always claims, "The early bird catches the worm."

4. Shakespeare once wrote better three hours too soon than a minute too late.

   Shakespeare once wrote, "Better three hours too soon than a minute too late."

5. From the sidelines, our coach shouts you can do it!

   From the sidelines, our coach shouts, "You can do it!"

6. Our teacher always states remember to turn in your homework.

   Our teacher always states, "Remember to turn in your homework."

Conquer Grammar • Grade 5 • © Newmark Learning, LLC

Page 57

Name _____ Date _____

Punctuation for Effect

Use an exclamation point at the end of a statement that shows strong emotion, such as excitement, surprise, happiness, or fear. Use a period at the end of a statement that does not show strong emotion.

I can't believe that I won first prize!
We are going to the pool today.

Circle whether each sentence shows strong emotion or not. Then write the correct end punctuation.

1. I'm thrilled that we got a puppy yesterday !

   (strong emotion) not strong emotion

2. It is my job to feed him in the morning .

   strong emotion (not strong emotion)

3. I was surprised when he licked my face !

   (strong emotion) not strong emotion

4. His tail wagged as I wiped my face clean .

   strong emotion (not strong emotion)

5. Never in my life have I seen a happier dog !

   (strong emotion) not strong emotion

6. After a family vote, we named him Julius .

   strong emotion (not strong emotion)

Conquer Grammar • Grade 5 • © Newmark Learning, LLC

Page 58

Name _____ Date _____

Punctuation for Effect

Use an exclamation point at the end of a statement that shows strong emotion, such as excitement, surprise, happiness, or fear. Use a period at the end of a statement that does not show strong emotion.

I can't wait to go to the beach!
I entered a pie in the baking contest.

Circle whether each sentence shows strong emotion or not. Then write the correct end punctuation.

1. We got so much rain yesterday .

   (strong emotion) not strong emotion

2. Ramona walked down the block .

   strong emotion (not strong emotion)

3. She couldn't believe she got caught in the rain !

   (strong emotion) not strong emotion

4. I brought my umbrella .

   strong emotion (not strong emotion)

5. I couldn't believe my eyes !

   (strong emotion) not strong emotion

6. Suddenly, a flash of lightning lit the sky !

   (strong emotion) not strong emotion

Conquer Grammar • Grade 5 • © Newmark Learning, LLC

Page 59

Conquer Grammar • Grade 5 • © Newmark Learning, LLC

Answer Key

Page 60

Capitalize Proper Nouns

A proper noun names a specific person, place, or thing. Each main word of a proper noun should begin with a capital letter. The titles and names of people, the days of the week and the months of the year, and specific holidays and names of geographic places are proper nouns.

On **Sunday, Marla** will visit the **Museum of Fine Art**.
Last **June**, the **Jones** family went to a beach in **New Jersey**.

Circle the proper nouns that should be capitalized. Then rewrite the sentence correctly. Underline any book titles.

1. Every (wednesday,) I go to (central library) after school.

   Every Wednesday, I go to Central Library after school.

2. One of the librarians is named (alicia morgan.)

   One of the librarians is named Alicia Morgan.

3. Miss (morgan) told me about a book sale next (saturday) afternoon.

   Miss Morgan told me about a book sale next Saturday afternoon.

4. Maybe I will find a book by (jerry spinelli,) my favorite author.

   Maybe I will find a book by Jerry Spinelli, my favorite author.

5. My older brother (wayne) likes (robinson crusoe) and other adventure classics.

   My older brother Wayne likes Robinson Crusoe and other adventure classics.

6. Once we buy our books, we will go to (finley park) to read them

   Once we buy our books, we will go to Finley Park to read them.

Page 60

Page 61

Capitalization in Dialogue

Quotation marks set off a speaker's exact words. Always capitalize the first word in the quotation marks. If the dialogue is interrupted, do not capitalize the first word in the continuation of the dialogue.

"**Let's** meet on the lower field today," said my coach.

Rewrite each sentence with correct capitalization.

1. Mr. Jefferson announced, "your rough drafts are due tomorrow."

   Mr. Jefferson announced, "Your rough drafts are due tomorrow."

2. "what is the topic of your research paper?" asked Ellie.

   "What is the topic of your research paper?" asked Ellie.

3. "the topic I chose is Rome," I said. "my grandfather lives there."

   "The topic I chose is Rome," I said. "My grandfather lives there."

4. Ellie wondered, "have you ever been there for a visit?"

   Ellie wondered, "Have you ever been there for a visit?"

5. "yes, but it's been a long time since I last visited," I answered.

   "Yes, but it's been a long time since I last visited," I answered.

6. "there are so many ancient ruins there," I shared. "it's hard to miss them."

   "There are so many ancient ruins there," I shared. "It's hard to miss them."

Page 61

Page 62

Capitalization and Punctuation in Titles

Capitalize the first word and each additional main word of a book or song title. Unless it is the first word of the title, do not capitalize **a**, **an**, and **the**, or most short prepositions, such as **at**, **in**, **by**, **for**, **of**, and **to**. Always underline a book, movie, or magazine title and place an article, poem, song, or story title in quotation marks.

Book title: I just read <u>Maniac Magee</u>.
Poem title: "A Spring Day" is a beautiful poem.

Underline or add quotation marks for the title in each sentence. Then rewrite the sentence with correct punctuation and capitalization for the title.

1. I borrowed big cats of south america from the library.

   I borrowed <u>Big Cats of South America</u> from the library.

2. Have you seen my book, chasing vermeer?

   Have you seen my book, <u>Chasing Vermeer</u>?

3. The article, island of the blue dolphins, is very informative

   The article, "Island of the Blue Dolphins," is very informative.

4. The author of survival in antarctica visited our school

   The author of <u>Survival in Antarctica</u> visited our school.

5. I bought intermediate camping tips to take on our trip.

   I bought <u>Intermediate Camping Tips</u> to take on our trip.

Page 62

Page 63

Capitalization and Punctuation in Titles

Capitalize the first word and each additional main word of a book or song title. Unless it is the first or last word of the title, do not capitalize **a**, **an**, and **the**, or most short prepositions, such as **at**, **in**, **by**, **for**, **of**, and **to**. Always underline a book, movie, or magazine title and place an article, poem, song, or story title in quotation marks.

Book title: <u>The Lightning Thief</u>
Song title: "America the Beautiful"

Rewrite each sentence with correct capitalization. Be sure to underline book titles and put quotation marks around song titles.

1. I just finished reading the best way to train a parrot.

   I just finished reading the article, "The Best Way to Train a Parrot."

2. I read a book called cooking and science and found out how the topics are similar.

   I read a book called <u>Cooking and Science</u> and found out how the topics are similar.

3. Our country's national anthem is called the star-spangled banner.

   Our country's national anthem is called "The Star-Spangled Banner."

4. I just bought the book, bridge to terabithia.

   I just bought the book, <u>Bridge to Terabithia</u>.

5. The first song I can remember singing is mary had a little lamb.

   The first song I can remember singing is "Mary Had a Little Lamb."

6. My mother's favorite mystery novel is a study in scarlet.

   My mother's favorite mystery novel is <u>A Study in Scarlet</u>.

Page 63

Answer Key

Page 64

Name _____ Date _____

Temporal Words

Temporal words and phrases signal the order in which events occur.
They make the timing of events clear.

Evan **first** went to the library and **then** he went home.
Yvonne went to the store **after** studying **for several hours**.

Underline the temporal word or phrase in each sentence.

1. The third time we went to the lake was the best.

2. What did we do two months ago?

3. An hour after we had lunch, we went back to the lake.

4. The village near the lake was established 100 years ago.

5. A year from now, I hope we will all meet here again.

6. We will be so happy when our friends arrive in a couple of hours.

7. I will set up for the picnic before they arrive.

8. I hope to be done one hour from now.

Rewrite each sentence. Add a temporal word or phrase to make the timing of events clear.
Sample answers are provided.

9. Do you want to walk the dog _____?

   Do you want to go walk the dog after lunch?

10. I have to go to the doctor _____, but I can join you before dinner.

   I have to go to the doctor after school, but I can join you before dinner.

64 Conquer Grammar • Grade 5 • © Newmark Learning, LLC

Page 64

Name _____ Date _____

Temporal Words

Temporal words and phrases signal the order in which events occur.
They make the timing of events clear.

I'm looking forward to seeing the movie **over the weekend**.
I hope we'll stop for pizza **after** the movie.
Did you know that it took **more than two years** to make this movie?

Underline the temporal words in each sentence.

1. We bought a special kite last week.

2. It took us many days to learn how to fly it.

3. After a short time, we were able to fly the kite successfully.

4. My sister and I kept that beautiful kite in the air for a while.

5. We read that the Chinese invented kites more than 2,000 years ago!

Rewrite each sentence. Add a temporal word or phrase to make the timing of events clear.
Sample answers are provided.

6. Aaron wanted to go swimming _____.

   Aaron wanted to go swimming before dinner.

7. Can you come to my graduation party _____?

   Can you come to my graduation party on June 21?

65 Conquer Grammar • Grade 5 • © Newmark Learning, LLC

Page 65

Name _____ Date _____

Temporal Words

Temporal words and phrases signal the order in which events occur.
They make the timing of events clear.

Can we go to the dog park **after school**?
I saw a great movie **last Saturday**.
Janie's parents moved to this country **fifteen years ago**.

Identify the temporal words or phrases in each sentence and write them on the line.

1. We went to a restaurant tonight after Mom got home. _tonight, after_

2. At first, we were going to drive, but then we decided to bike. _At first, then_

3. Ten minutes later, we arrived at our destination. _Ten minutes later_

4. I ordered a bowl of soup first, and next I ordered a burger. _first, next_

5. Our meals were on the table in just a few minutes. _in just a few minutes_

6. I would really like to eat there again on Friday night. _on Friday night_

Rewrite each sentence. Add a temporal word or phrase to make the timing of events clear.
Sample answers are provided.

7. Will you go to the amusement park _____?

   Will you go to the amusement park on Saturday?

8. We had a much worse hurricane _____.

   We had a much worse hurricane two years ago.

66 Conquer Grammar • Grade 5 • © Newmark Learning, LLC

Page 66

Name _____ Date _____

Sentence Fragments

A sentence fragment is an incomplete sentence that does not express a complete thought. It is missing a subject, a verb, or both. To correct a fragment, add the missing subject or verb.

Fragment: Crept along the shore.
Corrected: A **hermit crab** crept along the shore.
Fragment: The bird in the wind.
Corrected: The bird **soared** in the wind.

Circle whether the fragment is missing a subject or a verb. Rewrite the fragment as a complete sentence using one of the phrases below the fragment.

1. Planted lots of apple trees. (missing a subject, missing a verb)
   Farmer Brown   spent
   Farmer Brown planted lots of apple trees.

2. She the orchard with great care. (missing a subject, missing a verb)
   Julie   tended
   She tended the orchard with great care.

3. Some pumpkins from the farm fifty pounds! (missing a subject, missing a verb)
   Milly   weighed
   Some pumpkins from the farm weighed fifty pounds!

4. Awarded Farmer Brown a blue ribbon. (missing a subject, missing a verb)
   the judges   had
   The judges awarded Farmer Brown a blue ribbon.

5. Will she grow next season? (missing a subject, missing a verb)
   what   got
   What will she grow next season?

67 Conquer Grammar • Grade 5 • © Newmark Learning, LLC

Page 67

Answer Key

Name _____ Date _____

Sentence Fragments

A sentence fragment is an incomplete sentence that does not express a complete thought. It is missing a subject, a verb, or both. To correct a fragment, add the missing subject or verb.

Fragment: The cat its tail happily.
Complete sentence: The cat wagged its tail happily.
Fragment: Meowed when I filled its food dish.
Complete sentence: The cat meowed when I filled its food dish.

Circle whether the sentence is missing a subject or a verb. Then rewrite the sentence with a subject or verb that best completes the sentence.
Sample answers are provided.

1. I strawberry ice cream.　　　subject　　(verb)
   I love strawberry ice cream.

2. Contains many diagrams.　　　(subject)　　verb
   The book contains many diagrams.

3. Will have a math test next week.　　(subject)　　verb
   We will have a math test next week.

4. That birthday card very thoughtful.　subject　(verb)
   That birthday card is very thoughtful.

5. Why did leave?　　　　(subject)　　verb
   Why did she leave?

6. Who the person laughing?　　subject　(verb)
   Who is the person laughing?

68　　Conquer Grammar • Grade 5 • © Newmark Learning, LLC

Page 68

Name _____ Date _____

Run-On Sentences

A run-on sentence contains two or more complete thoughts. One way to correct a run-on sentence is to separate it into two or more sentences, each with a subject and a verb. Another way is to add a comma between the complete thoughts and a coordinating conjunction such as **and, but, or,** or **so.**

Run-on: The cat was orange and had white stripes it looked at its owner as it went to drink milk.
Corrected: The cat was orange and had white stripes**. It** looked at its owner as it went to drink milk.

Rewrite each run-on sentence as two complete sentences.

1. Here is a book that I would love to read it is about the wilderness.
   Here is a book that I would love to read. It is about the wilderness.

2. The first picture is of two bears in a river the water looks very cold!
   The first picture is of two bears in a river. The water looks very cold!

3. This chapter is about rivers some are in the West, while others are in the East.
   This chapter is about rivers. Some are in the West, while others are in the East.

4. In the next chapter, there is a picture of a bear its fur is shiny and thick.
   In the next chapter, there is another picture of a bear. Its fur is shiny and thick.

5. If I were a bear, I would climb up the tree quickly the branches look sturdy.
   If I were a bear, I would climb up the tree quickly. The branches look sturdy.

6. One page shows people hiking their packs look very heavy.
   One page shows people hiking. Their packs look very heavy.

Conquer Grammar • Grade 5 • © Newmark Learning, LLC　　69

Page 69

Name _____ Date _____

Run-On Sentences

A run-on sentence contains two or more complete thoughts. One way to correct a run-on sentence is to separate it into two or more sentences, each with a subject and a verb. Another way is to add a comma between the complete thoughts and a coordinating conjunction such as **and, but, or,** or **so.**

Run-on: The class read "The Legend of Sleepy Hollow" the students decided to perform it as reader's theater.
Corrected: The class read "The Legend of Sleepy Hollow**." The** students decided to perform it as reader's theater.

Rewrite each run-on sentence as two complete sentences.

1. We're sorry we arrived to your house late we were stuck in traffic.
   We're sorry we arrived to your house late. We were stuck in traffic.

2. The championship track meet was on all the runners ran so fast!
   The championship track meet was on. All the runners ran so fast!

3. Should I tell you the name of the book I think you would really like it?
   Should I tell you the name of the book? I think you would really like it.

4. I wrote down the recipe while we were watching the cooking show everything looked delicious and easy to make.
   I wrote down the recipe while we were watching the cooking show.
   Everything looked delicious and easy to make.

5. Ask your mom if you can come over we can study for our test.
   Ask your mom if you can come over. We can study for our test.

6. We'll make a good breakfast we just have to pick up a dozen eggs.
   We'll make a good breakfast. We just have to pick up a dozen eggs.

70　　Conquer Grammar • Grade 5 • © Newmark Learning, LLC

Page 70

Name _____ Date _____

Run-On Sentences

A run-on sentence contains two or more complete thoughts. One way to correct a run-on sentence is to separate it into two or more sentences, each with a subject and a verb. Another way is to add a comma between the complete thoughts and a coordinating conjunction such as **and, but, or,** or **so.**

Run-on: My dad prepared supper we ate it in an hour and then had dessert that I liked but my sister didn't because it was crunchy.
Corrected: My dad prepared supper**. We** ate it in an hour and then had dessert. **I** liked the dessert, **b**ut my sister didn't because it was crunchy.

Rewrite each run-on sentence as two or more complete sentences.

1. My brothers and I will go hiking this weekend and our father will take us to a local trail.
   My brothers and I will go hiking this weekend. Our father will take us to a
   local trail.

2. We need water to drink hydration is important when exercising.
   We need water to drink. Hydration is important when exercising.

3. I have hiked only once before hiking is very exciting.
   I have hiked only once before. Hiking is very exciting.

4. The trail is three miles and when we are hiking up the hill, we will be tired but when we go down, it should be easier.
   The trail is three miles. When we are hiking up the hill, we will be tired.
   When we go down, it should be easier.

5. The sun is shining brightly now maybe later it will be cloudy, which will make the day cooler.
   The sun is shining brightly now. Maybe later it will be cloudy, which will
   make the day cooler.

Conquer Grammar • Grade 5 • © Newmark Learning, LLC　　71

Page 71

Answer Key

Page 72

Name _____ Date _____

Sentence Fragments and Run-On Sentences

A sentence fragment does not express a complete thought. It is missing a subject, a verb, or both. To correct a fragment, add the missing subject or verb. A run-on sentence consists of two or more complete thoughts. One way to correct a run-on sentence is to divide it into two or more complete sentences.

Fragment: A flock of birds in a tree.
Corrected: We saw a flock of birds in a tree.

Run-on: They flew off when the wind shook the tree leaves fell down on us as we stood there watching the birds.
Corrected: They flew off when the wind shook the tree. Leaves fell down on us as we stood there watching the birds.

Determine whether each sentence is a run-on sentence or a fragment. Write the answer on the line.

1. The boy with a toy truck. _____fragment_____

2. Sipped from the straw. _____fragment_____

3. I have a younger sister who is two and she is great I love watching her learn to talk. _____run-on_____

4. The first word she said was "ball" and my father was so excited he whooped with laughter and so did I. _____run-on_____

Rewrite each run-on sentence as two or more complete sentences.

5. I squealed and said the word again everyone began to laugh.
   I squealed and said the word again. Everyone began to laugh.

6. I asked my father what my first word was and it was the very same word my sister had said and I was amazed!
   I asked my father what my first word was. It was the very same word my sister had said.
   I was amazed!

Page 73

Name _____ Date _____

Combine Sentences

Use the conjunction **and** or **or** to join the subjects (if the predicate appears in both sentences) or predicates (if the subject appears in both sentences) of two sentences.

Blair played on the tennis team. Jane played on the tennis team.
Blair **and** Jane played on the tennis team.

Combine each pair of sentences with the conjunction _and_ or _or_. Write the sentence on the line.

1. Strawberries are very nutritious. Blueberries are very nutritious.
   Strawberries and blueberries are very nutritious.

2. The Bears could win the tournament. The Lions could win the tournament.
   The Bears or the Lions could win the tournament.

3. My friend Maurice rode the roller coaster. My friend Tommy rode the roller coaster.
   My friends Maurice and Tommy rode the roller coaster.

4. Anna biked to the beach. Manuel biked to the beach.
   Anna and Manuel biked to the beach.

5. My mother likes to sing. I like to sing.
   My mother and I like to sing.

6. The balloons were for the party. The cake was for the party.
   The balloons and cake were for the party.

7. My dad might tell a scary ghost story. Dad's brother might tell a scary ghost story.
   My dad or his brother might tell a scary ghost story.

Page 74

Name _____ Date _____

Combine Sentences

Use the conjunction **and** or **or** to join the subjects (if the predicate appears in both sentences) or predicates (if the subject appears in both sentences) of two sentences.

The baby smiled widely. The baby giggled loudly.
The baby smiled widely **and** giggled loudly.

Combine each pair of sentences with the conjunction _and_ or _or_. Write the sentence on the line.

1. The storm rained out the softball game. The storm ruined the picnic.
   The storm rained out the softball game and ruined the picnic.

2. I might stay up late. I might go to bed early.
   I might stay up late or go to bed early.

3. I bike on Saturdays. I swim on Sundays.
   I bike on Saturdays and swim on Sundays.

4. The cat naps on the bed. The cat dozes in a patch of sun.
   The cat naps on the bed or dozes in a patch of sun.

5. The cup fell off the counter. The cup broke.
   The cup fell off the counter and broke.

6. The flight could be delayed one hour. The flight could be delayed two hours.
   The flight could be delayed one or two hours.

7. According to Bob, it should be hot today. It should be humid today.
   According to Bob, it should be hot and humid today.

Page 75

Name _____ Date _____

Compound Sentences

Use a comma and a coordinating conjunction such as **and, or, but, for, nor, so,** and **yet** to combine two sentences to make a compound sentence.

It was very hot, **so** it was difficult to run the cross-country workout.

Combine each pair of sentences to form a compound sentence. Use a comma and the correct coordinating conjunction.

1. Miguel twisted his ankle. He skinned his elbow, too.
   Miguel twisted his ankle, and he skinned his elbow, too.

2. He wanted to play in the game. His coach advised against it.
   He wanted to play in the game, but his coach advised against it.

3. Miguel wanted to disregard the advice. He actually agreed with it.
   Miguel wanted to disregard the advice, but he actually agreed with it.

4. Should he stay for the game? Should he go home instead?
   Should he stay for the game, or should he go home instead?

5. Miguel watched from the bench. His coach smiled in approval.
   Miguel watched from the bench, and his coach smiled in approval.

6. Miguel wanted to participate. He cheered the loudest for his team.
   Miguel wanted to participate, so he cheered the loudest for his team.

Answer Key

Name _____ **Date** _____

Complex Sentences

A complex sentence consists of an independent clause joined with a dependent clause by a subordinate conjunction. Subordinate conjunctions include **although**, **since**, **because**, **until**, **while**, **that**, **when**, and **where**. If the conjunction the sentence, place a comma between the clauses.

I did my homework in the library **until** it closed.
Although I worked steadily, I didn't finish the assignments.

Draw one line under the independent clause. Draw two lines under the dependent clause.

1. The fawn stayed close to the herd because there was a wolf nearby.

2. The herd was on high alert while the wolf remained.

3. The wolf gave up in exasperation since he could not approach the fawn.

4. Although the herd was nervous, it did not scatter.

Combine the two sentences to form a complex sentence. Use a subordinate conjunction from the box above.

5. Ants work together for survival. They are social insects.

   Ants work together for survival since they are social insects.

6. Ants are tiny. They are very strong.

   Although ants are tiny, they are very strong.

7. They follow the other ants in a line. This helps the ants find food efficiently.

   They follow the other ants in a line because this helps the ants find food efficiently.

Page 76

Name _____ **Date** _____

Complex Sentences

A complex sentence consists of an independent clause joined with a dependent clause by a subordinate conjunction. Subordinate conjunctions include **although**, **since**, **because**, **until**, **while**, **that**, **when**, and **where**. If the conjunction begins the sentence, place a comma between the clauses.

I shopped for clothes at the mall. It closed.
I shopped for clothes at the mall **until** it closed.

I had money to spend. I didn't buy anything.
Although I had money to spend, I didn't buy anything.

Combine the two sentences to form a complex sentence. Use a subordinate conjunction from the box above.

1. The author is coming out with a collection of short stories. I am not sure if I want to buy a copy.

   The author is coming out with a collection of short stories, although I am not sure if I want to buy a copy.

2. I had my rain boots. My feet and socks stayed dry.

   Because I had on my rain boots, my feet and socks stayed dry.

3. The weather is cold. I will wear this sweater.

   While the weather is cold, I will wear this sweater.

4. I won't go in the ocean. The water is cold and the waves are big.

   I won't go in the ocean because the water is cold and the waves are big.

5. The wind blew the trees. I walked through the park.

   The wind blew the trees when I walked through the park.

Page 77

Name _____ **Date** _____

Expand, Combine, or Reduce Sentences

Reduce sentences by deleting unnecessary words and phrases.
Expand sentences by adding important descriptive information.
Combine two sentences into one sentence.

Reduce: When I was ten years old ~~or maybe ten and a half~~, I learned to ski.
Expand: The traffic was terrible **on the highway**.
Combine: The traffic was slow, **but** we arrived in time. Allie wasn't in school today **because** she was ill.

Write whether the second sentence expands, combines, or reduces the first sentence or sentences.

1. a. The mother of my friend whom I knew from school saw to me first.
   b. My school friend's mother saw to me first.
   _____ reduces _____

2. a. It was a warm day. It was a windy day, too.
   b. It was a warm day, and it was windy, too.
   _____ combines _____

3. a. She liked how the petals of the flower that were wet shone in the sun.
   b. She liked how the flower's wet petals shone in the sun.
   _____ reduces _____

4. a. My aunt is loving.
   b. My aunt, who's in the kitchen, is loving.
   _____ expands _____

5. a. I'm glad that she made so many ice pops.
   b. I'm glad that she made so many ice pops in this heat.
   _____ expands _____

Page 78

Name _____ **Date** _____

Expand, Combine, or Reduce Sentences

Reduce sentences by deleting unnecessary words and phrases.
Expand sentences by adding important descriptive information.
Combine two sentences into one sentence.

Reduce: We drove ~~and I sat in the back seat~~ on curvy mountain roads.
Expand: I went to the baseball game **that was the winning game of the World Series!**
Combine: Traffic was heavy, **but** we still got there before the game started.

Rewrite each pair of sentences. Follow the instructions in the parentheses ( ) to expand, combine, or reduce the sentences.
Sample answers are provided.

1. The jaguar at the zoo had sleek fur. It had intense eyes.   (combine)
   The jaguar at the zoo had sleek fur and intense eyes.

2. My friend, who is named Clara just like her mother, sketched the gorillas. (reduce)
   My friend Clara sketched the gorillas.

3. The guide said not to take flash photos.   (expand)
   The guide who was leading the tour said not to take flash photos.

4. Nora waved her hands and waved her fingers at the lion cub.   (reduce)
   Nora waved her fingers at the lion cub.

5. The cub looked startled.   (expand)
   The cub looked startled and moved closer to its mother.

6. The guide said that the cub was very young. It likes to be near its mother. (combine)
   The guide said that the cub was very young, so it likes to be near its mother.

Page 79

Answer Key

Name _____ Date _____

Dictionaries

Use a dictionary to check the spelling, pronunciation, part of speech, and meaning of a word. Words in a dictionary are listed in alphabetical order, from **a** to **z**. Print dictionaries have two guide words on every page. The first guide word represents the first word on the page. The second guide word represents the last word on the page.

      Guide words: gadget • **gas**p
      Included on the page: game
      Not included: gather

For each pair of guide words, write _yes_ or _no_ to answer the question.

1. adamant • advancement
   Is the word **address** on this page? ___*yes*___

2. chairman • chowder
   Is the word **chute** on this page? ___*no*___

3. facility • fathom
   Is the word **fastener** on this page? ___*yes*___

4. lagoon • lava
   Is the word **laughter** on this page? ___*yes*___

5. necessary • neighbor
   Is the word **nervous** on this page? ___*no*___

6. pail • partner
   Is the word **panel** on this page? ___*yes*___

7. dog • domestic
   Is the word **donate** on this page? ___*no*___

8. service • setter
   Is the word **session** on this page? ___*yes*___

80   Conquer Grammar • Grade 5 • © Newmark Learning, LLC

Page 80

Name _____ Date _____

Dictionaries

Use a dictionary to check the spelling, pronunciation, part of speech, and meaning of a word. Words in a dictionary are listed in alphabetical order, from **a** to **z**. Print dictionaries have two guide words on every page. The first guide word represents the first word on the page. The second guide word represents the last word on the page.

      Guide words: sunshine • **sup**per
      Included on the page: super
      Not included: support

For each pair of guide words, write _yes_ or _no_ to answer the question.

1. charm • check
   Is the word **chatter** on this page? ___*yes*___

2. distaste • dive
   Is the word **district** on this page? ___*yes*___

3. official • old
   Is the word **optical** on this page? ___*no*___

4. spread • spruce
   Is the word **sprinkle** on this page? ___*yes*___

5. fair • fall
   Is the word **fare** on this page? ___*no*___

6. errand • establish
   Is the word **essay** on this page? ___*yes*___

7. vary • veil
   Is the word **vast** on this page? ___*yes*___

8. admit • adult
   Is the word **advance** on this page? ___*no*___

Conquer Grammar • Grade 5 • © Newmark Learning, LLC   81

Page 81

Name _____ Date _____

Homophones

Homophones are words that sound the same but have different spellings and meanings. Some examples include **there/their/they're**, **through/threw**, and **rap/wrap**.

    The pitcher **threw** the ball and it soared **through** the air.

Circle the two words that sound the same in each sentence. Then write the word that matches the definition.

1. If you have a cut on your (heel,) a bandage will help you (heal) quicker.
   Improve is another word for ___*heal*___.

2. The (principal) makes it a (principle) to treat all of the students kindly and fairly. **Chief** is another word for ___*principal*___.

3. Students are not (allowed) to talk (aloud) without raising their hand and being called on. **Permitted** is another word for ___*allowed*___.

4. The tourists (heard) that the (herd) of moose had moved to another area in the park. **Group** is another word for ___*herd*___.

5. (Whether) rain or shine, the (weather) won't stop us from weeding the garden.
   Either is another word for ___*whether*___.

6. The (seller) kept extra supplies in the (cellar) of the shop.
   Basement is another word for ___*cellar*___.

7. The mess at the (site) of the demolished building was an unpleasant (sight.)
   Location is another word for ___*site*___.

8. A dentist should treat all her (patients) with (patience.)
   Calmness is another word for ___*patience*___.

82   Conquer Grammar • Grade 5 • © Newmark Learning, LLC

Page 82

Name _____ Date _____

Homophones

Homophones are words that sound the same but have different spellings and meanings. Some examples include **peace/piece**, **flu/flew**, **wear/where**, and **new/knew**.

    Where did I leave the scarf I want to **wear**?

Circle the two words that sound the same in each sentence. Then write the word that matches the definition.

1. Val is going (to) try out for the school play, and I will, (too.)
   Also is another word for ___*too*___.

2. I see that (they're) at the kitchen eating (their) dinner.
   The word ___*they're*___ is a contraction.

3. My brother sometimes gets (bored) when we play a (board) game.
   Disinterested is another word for ___*bored*___.

4. (It's) fun to watch the kitten chase (its) toy.
   The word ___*its*___ is a possessive pronoun.

5. Salvatore felt (weak) for a whole (week) after being sick.
   The opposite of **strong** is ___*weak*___.

6. Michelle (threw) the basketball (through) the hoop and won the game.
   Tossed is another word for ___*threw*___.

7. Gerrold (knew) that the (new) action movie would be good.
   If you were aware of it, you ___*knew*___.

Conquer Grammar • Grade 5 • © Newmark Learning, LLC   83

Page 83

Answer Key

Page 84

Homophones

Homophones are words that sound the same but have different spellings and meanings. Some examples include **two/too/to**, **here/hear**, **deer/dear**, and **course/coarse**.

Incorrect: Those to games go in hear, to.
Correct: Those **two** games go in **here**, **too**.

Circle the correct word in the parentheses ( ) to complete each sentence. Then write the correct word for each definition.

1. The captain changed the (coarse, (course)) of the ship to avoid the storm.

   It means **direction**. _____course_____

   It means **rough**. _____coarse_____

2. We went to our local post office to (male, (mail)) our packages.

   It means a **man** or **boy**. _____male_____

   It means "send by post." _____mail_____

3. Sometimes she gets (board, (bored)) with historical fiction.

   It means **uninterested**. _____bored_____

   It is a piece of wood. _____board_____

4. Thanks, we received the two samples you ((sent,) cent).

   It is a unit of money. _____cent_____

   It means "moved something from one place to another." _____sent_____

5. We froze in our tracks, so that we wouldn't scare the (dear, (deer)) off.

   It is a hoofed animal. _____deer_____

   It is a greeting in a letter. _____dear_____

Page 85

Homophones

Homophones are words that sound the same but have different spellings and meanings. Some examples include **heard/herd** and **waist/waste**.

I **heard** from the farmhand that the **herd** was misbehaving.

Circle the incorrect word or words in each sentence. Then write the homophone of the word to make the sentence correct.

1. I'll get to my chores (write) away. _____right_____

2. In exactly (too) seconds, I'll start working. _____two_____

3. I (no) you (herd) me laughing before, but I'm ready to work now.

   _____know_____ _____heard_____

4. If I (eight) (sum) popcorn first, I might be more motivated. _____ate_____

   _____some_____

5. (Theirs) no need to frown. I won't (waist) any more time. _____There's_____

   _____waste_____

6. I am sure that I'll be (threw) in an (our.) _____through_____ _____hour_____

7. I can't (weight) to (bee) finished! _____wait_____ _____be_____

8. Tyler is deciding (weather) to help me the (hole) day. _____whether_____

   _____whole_____

Page 86

Homophones

Homophones are words that sound the same but have different spellings and meanings. Some examples of homophones include contractions and possessive pronouns like the following: **they're/their**, **it's/its**, **you're/your**, **who's/whose**.

Contraction	Possessive Pronoun
they're (they are)	their
it's (it is)	its
you're (you are)	your
who's (who is)	whose

Write the contraction for the words in the parentheses ( ) and its homophone on the correct line to complete each sentence.

1. _They're_ going to visit _their_ relatives for Thanksgiving. (they are)

2. Please lend me _your_ scooter if _you're_ not going to use it. (you are)

3. _It's_ important to keep our puppy on _its_ leash as we walk. (it is)

4. Dad told me, "I know _you're_ going to ace _your_ test today!" (you are)

5. _It's_ fun to watch our dog chase _its_ favorite ball. (it is)

6. _Whose_ pencil is this on the floor? _Who's_ missing a pencil? (who is)

7. My cat stares at _its_ food dish to let me know _it's_ hungry or thirsty. (it is)

8. _Their_ jerseys indicate what team _they're_ on. (they are)

9. _Whose_ book is that? _Who's_ missing a book? (who is)

Page 87

Informal and Formal Language

Informal language has a casual tone and consists of incomplete sentences and slang. Use informal language in friendly pieces of writing, such as an e-mail or a letter to a friend. Formal language consists of complete sentences and standard grammar. Use formal language in an essay or a letter to the editor. Avoid using contractions in formal pieces of writing.

Informal	Formal
Hey, want to grab lunch?	I wish to extend an invitation for lunch at noon.
Lou shouted, "Dude! It's been like forever since I saw you last!"	Lou said, "Hello, I have not seen you in a long time."

Circle whether each sentence has formal or informal language.

1. Wanna go to the mall after school?

   formal   ((informal))

2. I wish to file a complaint about the noise in our neighborhood.

   ((formal))   informal

3. Julio rolled his eyes at me, and I cracked up!

   formal   ((informal))

4. That guy was like, "Who, me?"

   formal   ((informal))

5. I would be grateful if you could send me details about your summer camp.

   ((formal))   informal

6. There is no way I'd ever see that scary movie.

   formal   ((informal))

Answer Key

Interjections and Informal Speech

Writers use informal speech in dialogue to indicate character and setting. They also often incorporate interjections, or short exclamations, to show a character's emotions, such as surprise or shock, excitement or fear. A strong interjection should end in an exclamation point. A comma should follow a mild interjection.

"**Yikes**, it looks as if we're **in for a real bad** storm," the lifeguard said.

Underline the informal speech or interjection in each sentence.

1. "Where are you going?" he hollered.

2. "Whoa," he said. "You're skating real fast!"

3. "Ain't a problem!" she shouted back gleefully.

4. "She acts as if it weren't nothin'," he said. "But she should cool it."

5. She skated around the block and back. "Gosh, that was fun!" she said.

6. "You're fixin' for trouble," he said.

7. Another skater zipped by. "Wow! Look at how fast he's goin'. I'm gonna catch up with him," she said.

Page 88

Interjections and Informal Speech

Writers use informal speech in dialogue to indicate character and setting. They also often incorporate interjections, or short exclamations, to show a character's emotions, such as surprise or shock, excitement or fear. A strong interjection should end in an exclamation point. A comma should follow a mild interjection.

Stop! Don't leave home without your wallet!
Hmm, where did I put my sunglasses?

Circle the informal speech or interjection in each sentence. Write *I* for informal speech, *S* for strong interjection, and *M* for mild interjection.

1. (Oh,) I didn't know you'd be shopping for gifts, too. ___M___

2. I'm (super kidding) about disliking shopping. ___I___

3. (Yikes!) These party decorations are hideous! ___S___

4. (Well,) do you like these gold and silver ones? ___M___

Rewrite each sentence with the interjection in the parentheses ( ). Be sure to use the correct punctuation for the interjection.

5. The train is pulling into the station. (hurry)

   Hurry! The train is pulling into the station!

6. I won the tournament. (wow)

   Wow! I won the tournament!

7. This book is overdue, so I'll return it to the library tomorrow. (well)

   Well, my book is overdue, so I'll return it to the library tomorrow.

Page 89

Interjections and Informal Speech

Writers use informal speech in dialogue to indicate character and setting. They also often incorporate interjections, or short exclamations, to show a character's emotions, such as surprise or shock, excitement or fear. A strong interjection should end in an exclamation point. A comma should follow a mild interjection.

Hey! I have **tons** of things to tell you.
Well, let's **hang out.**

Rewrite each sentence with an interjection. Choose from one of the following interjections: *Hurry, Stop, Wow, Hmm, Yum, Yikes, Yay.* Be sure to use the correct punctuation for the interjection.
Sample answers are provided.

1. That is the most awesome kite I've ever seen!

   Wow! That is the most awesome kite I've ever seen!

2. Let's hustle, or we'll miss our flight!

   Hurry! Let's hustle, or we'll miss our flight!

3. That ice cream was so delicious.

   Yum, that ice cream was so delicious.

4. I have so many chores to finish.

   Yikes, I have so many chores to finish.

5. I won the grand prize in the contest!

   Yay! I won the grand prize in the contest!

6. I wonder where you left your keys.

   Hmm, I wonder where you left your keys.

7. Don't skate on that ice! See the cracks?

   Stop! Don't skate on that ice! See the cracks?

Page 90

Precise Language

Use precise words or phrases to convey ideas in a clear way. Precise language makes a piece of writing more interesting because the reader is able to visualize what is being described.

General	Precise
The horse **ran** across the field.	The horse **galloped** across the field.

For each sentence, circle the words in the parentheses ( ) that are precise. Then write the complete sentence on the line.

1. Mr. Hirano (walked, (trudged)) along with the ((enormous) big) package.

   Mr. Hirano trudged along with the enormous package.

2. The child ((howled) cried) when he lost his (toy, (fuzzy bear)).

   The child howled when he lost his fuzzy bear.

3. A cat will often (make a sound, (hiss)) to (warn), tell) others that its angry.

   A cat will often hiss to warn others that its angry.

4. The (bad, (destructive)) toddler (went, (ripped)) through the toy store.

   The destructive toddler ripped through the toy store.

5. Bees (go, (buzz)) from plant to plant (looking for, (seeking)) pollen.

   Bees buzz from plant to plant seeking pollen.

Page 91